DREAM GIVER

BY

REV. EMMANUEL MUSINGA

Published by Purpose International Publishing USA

TABLE OF CONTENTS

INTRODUCTION

Why I Want to Write This Book

I am writing this book because I want to tell people about my life story - how I have been surviving my whole life and about my background. But I will never allow my past to affect my future. I wish to encourage other people who have been persevering through the pain their own life. It is possible to change your life even if you have been a victim in different problems. Do not give up the pursuit of your own life. You are the only one who will change your life. No one will work for you. You are the only one who can make you great. Be proud for who you are. Do not be ashamed of who you are.

I have a passion to help people who have struggled in different problems of life. I believe you and I are able to change our own life. What I believe is that the problems are not permanent. I want you, the one who will read this book, to understand that you have great challenges. You can change your life and achieve a great life. Forget what you have been going through. I want you to dream about your future. I want to let you think and dream freely. You own your own dream. Do not limit yourself. I want to let you know that you can dream bigger and change your life. Do not let your challenge own you. You need to be you and own your own life.

You can change your life by finding in your heart the passion you have. That is the gift God has given you. Passion can help you to do what God has been planning in your life. You need to believe yourself and do what you feel you have been called to. Do not allow anyone or anything to stop you from doing what you have been born to do.

You need to put your dream into action. Do not spend your time complaining. Spend your time by working on your dream. You need to work hard pursuing your future. Do not let anyone stop you from working hard for your dream. Along with the dream you want to do, you will find that your dream has enemy. Do not believe the word from your enemy to discourage you. Keep moving with your dream.

To be able to succeed with your dream, you need to have mentoring; someone who can help you to have enough information to keep moving on with your dream. Then you will be able to thrive with your dream. Your mentor will support you so that you do not quit on your dream. He will support you so that you can be successful. You need to think about your legacy; what you will leave behind when you are not here. Think how people will remember you. It is good to be remembered in a great way. And do not think that you are alone in this journey. There are many people who want to support you so that you can be successful.

Now you are doing a great thing by reading this book. While you are reading this book, have a pen and paper and write down your dream. Think about your future - how you can make changes in your life and how this can impact your life and others.

My passion is to help you succeed in your life so that you leave a legacy behind you. You are able to leave a legacy behind. Simply do the right thing and follow your passion. Do not fear your enemy nor negative people. You are who you are, and you need to know that God has a good plan for you - Ezekiel 29.11.

I want to let you know that as you are reading this book you are doing a great thing. It is your life. Take time for yourself. Read this book. Think about your life and where you will be in the future. What is your legacy? Take time and write down your dreams. Merely thinking about your future does not help you. Write down your dream and pursue it. You can change your life...and be thinking how you can impact other people.

I am taking this time to let you know that you can overcome any challenges you have been going through. I want you let know that you are greater and stronger than any problems you are going through. Do not live a life of fear. Fear is the word from the enemies of your life. Leave fear behind. Keep focusing on your dreams.

Your dream is your life. Do not allow anybody to take away your dream. I want to let you know that you are stronger than your fears and stronger than your enemies. You can be great and achieve greatly - if you think you can. Write down your dream and work for it. You will find many people who will support you and you will be great because you are thinking great. Yes, think great and you will be great, and you will achieve great things.

CHAPTER 1

My Story

I was born 1977 in Zaire, Africa; what you now known as the Democratic Republic of Congo. I was 20 when the new government changed the name to "Congo." I came from a family of nine siblings. My parents were farmers. My mother did not attend school, not even for one day. My father went to school until sixth grade. He did not continue because my grandfather did not know the importance of school. He asked my father to stay home and help him with the cows, since our business was cows. I remember when I was growing up, that taking care of cows was priority number one in our community. If you have many cows you are more respected in the community as a rich person.

When I was a young child we went to school without a pen or a book. I remember sometimes our class was under the trees. Life was really good; we didn't know any other life. I remember learning about bicycles in our village where there was no street. That was just life in our village. It was a fun life and we enjoyed it. We didn't know about any life "on the other side." We would walk two to three hours to get to school.

I started school in the 1st grade when I was around eight years old because the school was far away. You can't start school if you're too young. You couldn't walk that far. We didn't have preschool, so we stayed home with parents. Plus, in school there wasn't food, so many children who live in the village cannot start school at an early age.

Around 1990 I was sick with malaria. My cousin, a grown man, told me with calm assurance that he had malaria medicine for me. Well I was a child and I trusted him. I trusted him as he injected me with expired medicine using a cow syringe! Then around nightfall I start feeling tremendous pain and swelling. I had a bad infection. Night after night I laid awake on my bed in so much pain. I stayed in bed for two weeks. In the third week my father told me he wanted to treat me for this infection. So, he took his knife, and put it in a fire until it became red hot. After he cut through the swelling, he took water and cleaned out all the infection. I was really in pain. But one week later I was walking normally, and everything was fine. We did not have any hospital or clinic; we were just living in the village without any healthcare or electricity. There was not clean water either as we drank water from the river.

My father, with the boys, would focus on taking care of the cows and cutting trees. Whereas my mother planted the corn and beans and cared for the house. All the boys in the village worked closely with their fathers. The parents put the boys first. We did not have a gender equality situation. All boys must go to school while girls must stay home with their mothers and help them. The job of women in the house is: clean the house, take care of the kids, farm to bring food home, and cook food for the father and boys. I did not know any boys who could cook. I am glad now that some of our community is starting to understand the importance of equal value in each gender.

My father and my mother
Rabun Rupande and Ramu Nyirankema

This is my older brother.
Biregeya Fabien Rupande

I want you to see the life we used to live. As boys you must know how to milk a cow by the age of fifteen and marry around the age of sixteen. Also, boys and fathers must protect the farm from the monkeys that liked to eat so much of our corn. Corn is our first food. We prepared it with milk. We needed to make sure, we had plenty of corn in the house as it is our food. And we had to wake up in the morning before the monkeys wake up. We went to the farm with our dogs and made a fire. When the monkeys saw us around the fire with our dogs, they knew they could not eat corn from our farm. We had to do all this for a period of three month while there were standing corn stalks. In our community all marriages were arranged marriages. Your father and mother would choose who you married. I remember seeing my father and mother discuss my brother's fiancés. My two brothers married according to whom my parents chose. That was the culture we were living among. For us it was normal life.

PASTOR EMMANUEL
MUSINGA RUPANDE

Around 1999 I was shot in my left leg. When I got to the General Hospital in Bukavu, the first medical opinion I heard was that they had decided to take off my left leg. I start crying. But before they could operate, my father came and took me to the Rwandese Hospital. At first, he did not have a way to take me there. But I realized that he must have thought of something for he took me in a truck for 145 km/90+ miles. When we got to the University Hospital in Butare, Rwanda, I met with one Doctor who was teaching at the University. He was from Germany. His name was Doctor Janice Bakeoff. He is the doctor that saved my leg. I stayed in the hospital six months. I started learning how to walk again with crutches. I did not go back to my country.

Around 2001 my father encouraged me to go back to school. There was a great opportunity to go back to school though it was hard for him to pay school fees for us all - my three brothers, my sister, plus myself.

Then sadly my father was diagnosed with cancer. He went to the hospital for treatment, but he did not recover. He died 02 December 2002. Gloom settled over me as I lost hope for my life and my family. We stayed with our mother though she did not have a job. Remember, she had never been to school, and did not have any marketable skills that could give her any job. What is worse, among my brothers and I, no one had a high school diploma. We could not get any job. Life quickly became very hard. At that time, my older brother and two other brothers were living in Congo. Yet my mother and I, with the other siblings, were living in Rwanda. Many hungry nights passed. And to make things worse, we could not afford school.

Then I started working afternoons while going to school in the morning. I started to care for my family as if I were the head of the family. Life had become very laborious for me and my siblings. At times when we did not pay school fees, the teachers said they could not keep us in the classroom. It is true. They kicked us out of class many times because we could not afford school fees. So, I kept working to provide food and pay the school fees. Then some anonymous good people offered to help us long term and World Vision paid the school fees for my younger brothers and sister. In time, one brother and I both graduated high schools. It was my dream to be a lawyer, so I enrolled at Law University at Kigali, Rwanda. Though I was happily pursuing a law career, my heart was changing. Though I was going to Law School I started having the passion to be a minister. It kept growing in my heart. Part of me did not like this because it was my dream to be a lawyer. Then in the course of time I did not have money to pay the fees for law school. I decided to go to Kenya and report myself to the United Nations as a refugee. Maybe I would be able to get help this way. I was thinking maybe I would be able to continue the school.

I arrived in the ethnic minority community called Banyamulenge, Tutsi. Because of the racial discrimination from other ethnics in the refugee camp, the United Nations accepted us as urban refugees in Nairobi. That is why they allowed me to stay in Nairobi under the protection of the United Nations. It was then and there that I started learning English. I clearly remember that time. It was 2005. At this time, I knew only two words in English! But I really wanted to learn and very much so. I was very eager to be hearing English in school and to be writing English.

Although I still have my accent, I was learning English. Indeed, I was even speaking English. I joyfully walked two hours - seven miles each day to learn English. There was two hours of daily learning, then two hours walking back. I started working helping one family with cooking. My salary was $35 per month. That way I could pay various expenses, pay transportation, and pay enough to stay in school. It was not easy for I did not eat any lunch at school. I could not afford it.

I continued my schooling and learning English. I was so glad to be in school. I kept thinking about my future. I did not have any immediate dream to pursue, though I kept thinking about my life. At this point I did not believe in myself, not yet. I did not know the purpose of my life. When I started thinking about my life as a refugee boy without parents, hungry, broken, and hopeless, I could not believe that I could achieve anything great. But then again, look how far I had come since then! Then one fateful day, I had an extra $1. I saw a DVD of Dr. Martin Luther King and I bought it. I gazed at it for two hours while walking back home. This DVD quickly changed my thinking. That is why I really liked his speech so much. It was my first time to hear the speech, "I have a dream."

Before this, no one had ever told me anything about having a dream or pursuing a dream. So, I started thinking about my dream, and how I can change my life and help my family. Another big event happened one day when I was on the bus. I saw a lady reading Dr. Myles Munroe's book called *The Purpose of Living*. I asked this lady if I could borrow her book. I badly needed to read it. I told her that I needed to read Dr. Munroe's book because I did not know my purpose of my life. She agreed so I followed her to her place where she loaned me this book for two weeks. I read it feverishly, going through it twice then brought it back to her home. Since then the book, *The Purpose of Living*, blessed my brain and opened my mind. I must say that since reading Dr. Munroe, I know who I am.

It was 20 December 2008 that I got married to my wife Clementine Musinga. We were a refugee boy and girl who did not even have money for a honeymoon. But we really have strong love, committed hearts and a great relationship.

Today we have a big family of four children: one boy and three girls. We are very busy and happily enjoying our American life as we pursue our dream every single day.

Reverend Emmanuel R. & Clementine Musinga

We started our life together with nothing but hope and a big dream. I started working in a restaurant when we married. From the start I was telling her my big dreams; how I would be planting churches, continuing my school in the US, and that I would be a motivational speaker. She simply believed me, and we started a church in Nairobi, Kenya right away. We borrowed money to build the church building. From the beginning we never doubted God.

It was 2009 when I started the ministry. My passion to preach the gospel deepened when I saw the need in the refugee community. More were coming from Congo. They cannot understand English nor Swahili very well, so we started teaching Bible to them in our language. Then we started a church for them. I was senior pastor as well as working in the restaurant. I have been working as a volunteer pastor ever since. I have been working in different jobs to support my family. It is not easy, but I have been busy every single minute to make sure I keep moving forward with my dreams. For I believe in dreams. This may be easy for you or it may be difficult. But it is possible. You can achieve any dream you want to achieve.

Reverend Emmanuel Musinga

On 09 December 2010 I was granted resettlement; permission to move to America. The Federal Government moved me to Rock Island, Illinois. It is a small city and that is where we started our journey in America. I came through the organization called World Relief. Their case worker was helping us with orientation, and teaching us the basic things in American life; housing, how to take the bus, and how to fill out a job application and to make sure we get a job before we run out of benefits. One must know that if you come to America as a refugee you get rent for six months. Then after six months you must start to pay your own bills and you are required to pay back the airline ticket.

Mike & Julie Gray

I met this beautiful couple who invited me to their church called Wildwood Church. The Grays, and many others in this church, became part of my family at Wildwood. Many members of this church took their time teaching American life to us including shopping. Many people who are born in the USA do not understand the other side of the world. If you have not yet gone to other countries, you cannot understand how it is to learn everything anew as soon you land in the USA. It was very special as they started to teach me how to drive. In my entire family I am the first one who had ever owned a car or gotten a driver's license!

Mike Gray and Emmanuel Musinga

The photo showing Mike Gray and me is the day that
Mike took me to the DMV Rock Island to take the driver's
license test. I was happy beyond what you can imagine. This
is my favorite picture in my whole journey of life so far. This
was my first success. It was a dream for a long time, even back
when I was a child. I believed that one day I would own my
own car and drive it myself. That someday had come when
Wildwood Church donated a car to my family, and I started
to drive my family. That was a dream come true. I believe God
will help me to achieve all my dreams. I work every single day
so that I can support my dream and my family.

I got my first job in the USA doing maintenance at Wal-
Mart. My duty was cleaning everywhere in the Wal-Mart
and cleaning all the bathrooms and stocking the towels and
toilet paper. That was my first job in America, and I enjoyed
it. As long as I could support and provide food and housing
to my family things were good. My wife was working at the
Tyson meat processing plant. Before we had a car, we took the
bus. We found daycare care where we could leave our children.
We used to take three buses to get to daycare. My wife
would leave early in the morning to work. Then I took the
children on the bus to daycare in route to my work. Then in
the afternoons she went on the bus to get them, transferring
repeatedly. It was very tiresome. Then after the Wildwood
Baptist Church gave us a car that spared my children from
six bus rides per day…in winter! God bless the members of
Wildwood Church.

Honestly, it was fun to drive. Then one day I was speeding.
When the police pulled me over, I was scared to death. I did
not know why he was pulling me over. I started thinking, "Am
I going to jail? Do I leave my kids behind?" What will my
wife do?" Just then I remembered what my friend Mike Gray

told me that you must keep your hands on the wheel if the police pull you over. So, I kept my hands on the wheel.

When he told me to put the window down? I did. I was so frightened I asked him, "Sir, are you taking me to jail?"

He said, "No, do you know why I pulled you over?"

I said, "No sir." Then he told me I was speeding. I did not know I was speeding. I assured him I was sorry. I honestly did not know I was speeding. He asked for my driver's license. After I gave it to him, he went back in his car for a bit. There I was enjoying my first car - not thinking about speeding. But then he gave me a ticket. Since that time, I started to watch the speed limit. Before I did not.

Back in the time of President Mobutu's regime, we were scared of the police because he did not pay the police. They paid themselves by taking money and valuables from the population during traffic stops. We had learned that when you see Mobutu's police, run from them! If you did not, they would take anything you had. Thankfully, my friend Mike Gray taught me to not run away from the police. For if you run, they may think you are criminal and could mistakenly shoot you. That was totally different from my upbringing and why it is very hard for us to understand at first. We need to cooperate with the police. Praise God we have a program for the community where Wildwood and Trinity church together teams up to bring in police to speak about public safety. It is so helpful.

In 2011 I started having ideas and looking where I can go to do more, to jumpstart my life, raise my children for more productivity, and to establish myself better. Then late November of that year I was invited to speak in the

Congolese church of Dayton, Ohio. I went there realizing "I can drive on highways too!" Though I was still new in America, someone was driving me before now. Up to then I merely drove work to home to church or the store. During this drive, it was my first time to see Indianapolis. My heart told me that this was the place I needed to live with my family. I did not know a single person in Indiana. I searched to find anyone I knew but did not find a soul. Because of this, it took time to convince my wife to move to Indianapolis. But we moved to Indianapolis 03 June 2012. I was looking for a place to call "home" and Indianapolis was it! I love it here. Indiana is my "home state." I love finding what I was looking for in life. In terms of a location, everything I was missing in life I found it there.

We first started our church in Indianapolis 24 December 2012. With only a few members, we would use another church's sanctuary shortly after they were done with their service. We moved to different places to save money. During this time of searching we even used our own apartment because it was always too expensive to rent or too busy elsewhere. Finally, we were in our own building by early July 2013. We thanked God for Crooked Creek Baptist Church as they welcomed us in their building. We used their building for worship, and they gave me an office space for my studies!

It was a great miracle for all Congolese refugees of Indianapolis. We honor God as we use this building for many community meetings, church meetings, weddings and more. It was marvelous provision from God for us. Before we met the dear people of Crooked Creek Baptist, I remember numerous times crying out, asking God, "Why do you give me this passion when you know what we need? Can you not connect me with the right people who understand what we have been going through?" Finally, God answered our prayers. We truly appreciate Crooked Creek Church. My heavens have they ever been a tremendous blessing to our community! And since the Federal Government has brought more Congolese refugees to Indiana, our community has been growing every day. We have so many people who have never been to school, not even one day. But everyone from Congo works and pays up, building his life and pursuing his dream. Many of them own their own houses already.

Looking back, this is how we used to live in the village in Congo. We really enjoyed ourselves. We did not know any other life. There was no hospital, no clean water. We used to bring water from the river a couple miles away. It was hard to have enough water in the house. With no electricity we were always living in the dark each night. It was hard to see. We drank milk as that was the first food, we all had. We milked cows with our own hands and fingers. All the community was living the same life. Everybody was feeling good because we did not know any other life.

We had moved here to this part of Congo because of civil war. No one dreamed that one day we would be in America living another life altogether. Being on this side of the world, I can still look back and remember when my father told me that if you work hard, you can live the good life you want. He also told me that it's possible, if you put your time in, that the key to living a good life requires focusing on your education. That statement from my father made me like school so much. It started me thinking about how I can help my family leave this kind of poor life we are living. I also wanted to help my community to entirely change our mindset. Too often we think that "the good life" belongs to some other people - that we are not able to live a good life like others. But me, I believed what my father told me. Though I did not have a high school diploma back then, I felt in my heart that I must fight this poverty in my family and in my community. I believed it was possible to change course. My first motivation was that I did not want my children to live the life I used to live. I did not want my wife to have our babies in the bush.

My mother, God bless her, she used to labor and deliver us children in the house and in the bush. Wanting better motivated me to work hard every day and to learn English. In my mind I resolved to fight the great spiritual enemy who had taken over my family and my life. It was then, in 2003, that I started dreaming about moving to America. My father had already passed. I did not have another choice. I must work hard to change our lives or accept this life, die as a poor boy in a poor family without education.

With this renewed mindset, I was going to school in the morning and going to work in the afternoon. All the money I made was for food and paying school fees for me, my brothers, and sister. Today everyone in my family has a high school diploma. I want to assure you that everything is possible if you put your time in. A good life is there for everyone who decides to work for it.

I remember the words of my father's last breath. He told me, "Please, take care of your family." Neither he nor I wanted my mother to die with sorrow. Right there I decided in my heart to take care of my brothers, my sister, and my mother. My father died from cancer. During that season we did not have food in the house. He was so sick when he would ask my mother to give him some food. But we did not have anything in the house. It was a really bad situation with my father sick.

We needed to take care of him. He used to tell us that he was going to die soon, and we needed to finish school to have a better life. He asserted, "If you don't continue your education, you will never have a better life. Keep living in the city. Do not go back to the village after I am no longer here. Keep trying in life and one day you will have better life."

This is me and my family as we are telling my father "goodbye." These are literally the last minutes of his life. It was this day that I realized that I need to work hard for my own life. No one else will care about my life since the one I relied upon and who cared about me was gone now. I knew 'the game' was now in my hand. At first, I did not know what to do. I always thought my father would make a good life for us. But now he was gone, I did not have thoughts about any another way to live. I did not know how my siblings and I would go forward. We were hopeless that day.

And then I started reading the Bible. I did not quit. I kept going to school and working to make sure we had food on the table. Many times, we were hungry. There was no food in the house, and we needed to finish homework because we had tests coming up at school. That is difficult to do when you are hungry. In these times you must have great determination. It was 2003, and I was determined to change my life and my family's life.

I remember my high school teacher telling us about Dr. Martin Luther King. He would tell us about American life. Eventually I met some people who had been in America. I asked them about living in America. They told me how American people are living. It was a good life. They have peace and goodness and freedom. That was the day I started dreaming about coming to America. I began telling my mother and my siblings, "Don't worry. Even though father has died, I will take care of you. We will be successful. One day you will forget this grim life we are living."

I began to tell my family that I will one day have enough money and we will have enough food in the house and wear good clothes. I said this to comfort them because we had not had good food in the house for a long time. That day my younger brother (the last born) did not believe me. He had many questions. I told him I would work hard and one day I will be in America as a successful man. He had his doubts and that was okay.

My first dream was to speak English. I moved from Rwanda, then through Uganda to Kenya. I started learning English. By now it was 2005. At the start I knew only two phrases of English, "How are you?" and "Good morning". I worked hard to learn English. As a refugee in Kenya I started the process for resettlement to move to America. This took me five years. When I moved here, I left my mother in Africa. We were separated, my mother and the other siblings. Finally, my mother joined me in the USA in 2016, after we had been separated for 6 years.

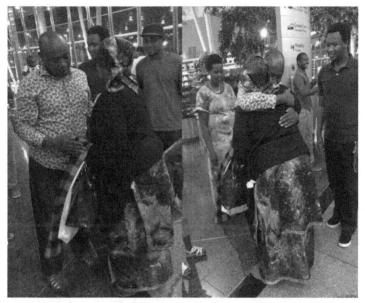

Here I am welcoming my mother at the Indianapolis Airport after being separated for six years. I used to send money to her in Africa to pay bills. I love my mother so much. She is my hero. She supported my dream and encouraged me always. As soon as I was living in the USA, my dream was to bring my mother to me in America. I was very happy to see my mother again. It was my plan to see my mother one day in America. She arrived when nearly 70 years old. It makes me so happy to see the life she is living now. My biggest dream was to give her a good life in her old age.

She would talk of growing up in her Congo village. She worked hard every day to raise the children, take care of the farm, and make sure we had food on the table. She delivered all her nine children either in the house or in the bush, sometimes by herself, sometimes with a midwife. I see her as my hero. Even after my father died, every day she still encouraged us to keep loving school and behaving good. She would teach us to be a good Christian and be good boys in the community. She allowed for no one to go to jail or live a bad life. She was a really great mother. Even at times when we didn't have food in the house she would keep telling us to not worry, that one day life will be better. She always, said, "Don't misbehave, always be nice, and God will bless us one day." I remember she told me that our father was a good person, a fine pastor who served God and helped people. Today I too am a servant of God. And I believe me that one day we will see the glory of God in this house, and in Him we will have everything we desire.

My family with Dennis & Kim Ford

Dennis Ford and his wife Kim accompanied me in welcoming my mother at the Airport. They have been longtime friends since 2011. Very soon after moving to the USA, the Fords became my friends. So, they came to rejoice with me when I was welcoming my mother. Looking back, I was living in sorrow. My father died without ever seeing my children. My mother she was living far away in Africa. She had never seen my children. At Indianapolis Airport it was the first time for her to see her grandchildren. Everyone was so excited to see each other. I was so happy to see my mother hug my children. Then finally I got to hug my mother. I told mother I was so glad to see here again. It was wonderful to see my dream come true. She has abundant time with grandchildren. My wife and I are able to work. And we can afford all we need. It is also wonderful for everyone that our children are with family, my mother, instead of daycare. This gives them extra time together.

I am grateful to God for the opportunity to work hard every day. My wife and I work multiple jobs to be able to pay our bills. I work two jobs plus do pastoral ministry. It is such a great opportunity to be in America. Every day I see opportunity around me. I love working any job you can imagine. I had known a different life. I did not want to keep living that same life. I wanted to go upward to the next level of living. I know it is not easy to be successful, but it is possible in America, and the better path is clearly open to anyone who tries. Many American people do not see it and believe it, and that is sad. But for people like us who have been in other countries, when you land in America, you see millions of opportunities. When I arrived in America, I started to dream of owning my own house. So, I built a five-bedroom house for my wife and children. When I see my girls joyful and in a good neighborhood, I feel peace in my heart. And I will keep working hard every day of my life to make sure my children live a good life. I am determined to leave a legacy for them.

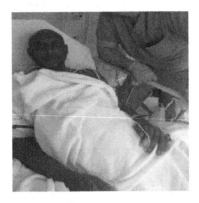

Around 2013 I was diagnosed with cancer. Going through chemotherapy was a huge challenge for my family. It seemed everything was going wrong. Cancer hit during these first three months living in Indianapolis. We did not have any friends. Though life did not seem good to me and my family, I tried to l keep encouraging my wife and telling her that I will be healed. I still had a lot of things to do, so I trusted God was going to heal me. God blessed me with such a great wife. She took care of me, kept working and paid the bills. I remember she managed to suspend our paying rent for a year. She had secured a loan that we paid back with interest along with our rent. My wife was strong and clever even though things were very bad. Simply seeing my daughters made me cry thinking how my children would struggle to survive if I died. Visions of my father's death kept coming back. But after chemotherapy, I was cancer free. Praise God. He had given me another opportunity to live long in service to Him and helping others. Newly healed I resumed working hard again. I am so eternally amazed at how God is using American doctors to treat different diseases. I am back on track again with my dreams after surviving cancer. Wife and I became excited as we started saving toward buying a house.

I remember when we first went to a real estate agent to ask how to buy a house. We asked the gentleman who welcomed us in his office how we could buy a house. He then asked us, "Do you have credit?" I was puzzled. What was credit? And he told me that we needed to build credit. I asked him how to build my credit. He told me that you need to have a credit card. When I showed him my debit card, he laughed. It was a funny exchange. Then he explained to me that it was not a credit card. After this I started learning how to build credit in preparation for getting a home.

Making corn flour

Back in Congo this is how we made corn flour, the primary food in our community. We did not have machines for making corn flour or cassava flour. We used the trees to make our own food. This life was fun and good. People still live this life. You could find a machine to make the flour, yet the people use their wisdom and resort to other solutions. I clearly remember growing up in this life. I used to help my mother make corn flour. It was hard work. In Congo today this is how living is for millions of people.

This how we used to wash clothes, take showers, and fetch water to bring home

This river is where we all used to wash our clothes by hand. No one had a washing machine nor even knew what a washing machine was. I too never saw or heard of one until I came to America. We would also shower/bathe in this river. Yes, it was normal to bathe in the river outside. It was not questionable. It was not humorous. No one would laugh at you or see it as something wrong. Everyone bathed in the river.

And the river was where we got water to drink and to cook with. For the parents and elderly who could not walk the miles to shower in the river we carried water from the river to home. For some it was a mile or even two. But we must provide that. We did not have a choice. Most of the time, children and women do that job of bringing water home. In my former village, that is the life they are still living now. I dream maybe one day I will be able to do something for my community. We need more people who have a passion to change lives.

My father's house

This house was my father's house. It had three bedrooms: one was for the girls, another for the guests and a master room. There was also a sitting room with wooden chairs. This is where my father would welcome his guests.

These were the houses where our family grew up.

We grew up in these houses. My father's house was the big house. Another we all used was the kitchen. All the boys would sleep in the same house. My older brother was living with his wife in another house. The cows had their place behind that house. Though I live in Indiana today, this place was my childhood where I grew up. Frankly, I miss it.

We did not have electricity in the house; we used the firewood to cook and to make the house warm. We did not

have clean water. And there were not bathrooms in the house
– in any of them.

Women carrying things is our transportation. And this
picture is how we would carry them. We walked long days.
That was the only way we knew to take things from market or
anywhere to home.

We walked over mountains and were always carrying items.

There were not streets or cars to help us to take things home.
You had one choice - to carry things yourself and take them
where you want to go. This is the life I used to live. In many
ways' things are easier now. Yet as I keep pursuing another life
in Indiana, maybe I will be able to help my people in Congo
one way or another.

Again, this is how we do our transportation.

Women carry things on their head. Anytime they want to go anywhere or bring food home, they must carry it on their head. This is the life we used to live, I too used to carry everything on my head and walk many miles.

I was so happy to pass my test to become a U.S. citizen.

28

I am so proud of my wife Clementine. When we came to America, she did not speak English and I was worried about her. We did not have time to go to school to learn English. We had to work so that we were able to pay bills. I was concerned about her passing the test of citizenship. But she learned English, and she studied and here she is. She passed the test and is now an American citizen.

Here is the Musinga family, so proud to be American citizens together as a family. It was my biggest dream to come to America and change my family's life. I did not want my children to languish and suffer the life that I did. I did not want my wife to deliver our children in the bush like my mother. I did not want my children to be refugees – hopeless like I was. My time spent reading the Bible and praying and asking God to make a way for me to change my life paid off. I am glad I am here in America and an American citizen. The test was not easy, but I was so excited to do this test. And because I was excited and prepared, I passed the first time.

American people, do not you ever take America for granted. You are fortunate to be born in American or to live in this country. You have freedom and plentiful opportunities around you living in this great country. You can do what you want to do and be what you want to be. Billions of people around the world are missing out and doing without. There is no food on the table, no education available, and no facilities. In America, a bus takes you to school and, if you need it, you are fed at school! I cannot understand anyone who, with these opportunities, does not have a high school diploma.

I was so warmed at heart when I was granted citizenship. When we grew up in our village in Congo, I did not know that you could become another citizen from another country. When I was young, I did not know there were other countries. I came from the Banyamulenge ethnicity. Citizenship is a thorny issue in Congo. My ancestors had been in Congo, long before the colonization of when King Leopold came to Congo from Belgium. My ancestors were living in Congo, when western countries divided Africa, and even before the Portuguese came to Africa. Even back then, we were there. But I also learned that our ancestors are also Tribal Tutsis from Rwanda. It is wearisome that communities have been fighting because of tribal matters that were not meant to be a problem.

That being said, I am glad now that I am an American citizen. I still love my home country of D. R. C. Congo, but I am proud to be an American citizen as my second home.

CHAPTER 2

How People Get a Dream

A dream is somewhere you want to go or something you want to do but you have not achieved it yet.

A dream is something living in your mind. You see it in your vision, but you do not have it in your hands yet - though you have it in your mind.

What you dream of is your future. Without a dream, you will never have a great future. Your dream today is your life tomorrow. Anything that you will have in your pocket or in your hands will first reside in your mind. Everything starts in your mind. Then you have it in your hands.

To make your dream clear you must know and understand the difference between mission and vision. Your vision makes you different from others.

The mission is common many people have some mission that they live by. We must know very well our mission and understand it. We will meet many people who have some sort of a mission like you. It is always helpful to relate and learn from them because in ways you have some mission and goals that could benefit from interacting with them.

Examples: All restaurants have a mission to feed people. Just as all churches have a mission to preach the gospel as they perceive it. It is common to have a mission.

Vision, however, is unique. You must understand that you are different from others. And it's your vision for YOUR destiny that makes you different from others.

The vision of a Chinese restaurant is a buffet. That makes them different from other restaurants. But their mission (common to all restaurants) is to feed people. To the level that you understand your vision, know that it is what makes you different. Your vision for your life is distinctive. It will be what makes your life unique.

You must know the difference between these 4 things

Job/occupation - is something you do to make a living whether it's your passion or not. Sometimes you may not even like your job, but you keep doing it. It supports you while on the journey toward your passion. A job is something you do because they pay you. Without the salary, you can't do it any longer.

Work - is something you were born to do. You like it, even without payment you keep doing it. There is a lot of work we do that we aren't paid for. Yet you enjoy doing it always.

Desire - is something you want to do because you can make money. You may find such an opportunity through a friend or associate. It can even be a temporary job; you may do it though not for life. But because you can make more money on it you want to do it while working toward your passion. You may be learning something or because you can finish soon or make quick cash. But in this be careful because many people who follow their desire kill their passion without realizing it.

Passion is something you love and you enjoy doing it. Even when it's very challenging you keep doing it. It likely feels like love versus work. Even if you don't earn enough money on it but you keep at it because of the joy it brings you. If you keep doing what you love, you keep enjoying your life every day.

Six Ways People Receive Dreams

1) By thinking

Dreams come by thinking about the purpose of your life. God has made us with a wonderful purpose to be in this world. It's not an accident that we are here. It doesn't matter how, by whom, or where you were born. You are still in the plan of God since you are here. Now, it's your responsibility to find and discover your purpose for being on this earth. Face the fact that you are great and that you will be successful if you take time and think about your life.

God has given to us 3 great things:

A) We have a memory. And we can remember everything once distractions are removed. Memories play again in your brain so think about them. When we remember victories, we believe God can again give us victory any time we ask him. When David went to fight Goliath he remembered those first victories. I Samuel 17:33-36 that is why we remember things, we can replay our victories and believe God according to what we have learned.

B) Imagination is something God has given to his people. We can imagine where we can be and where God can take us, and what we can do in our life. Imagination is the gift God gives to all people made in His Image. Everything you imagine is possible if you believe it and put your time in on it. Dr. Mike Murdock said if your heart decides where to go, your mind will create a map of how to get there.

Your mind is your garden. You can plant every seed and it can grow. Everything you teach your mind becomes possible to understand and do. Everything you decide to believe, your mind is able to accept and embrace. Your mind is your "genius engine" that works for you. In life there are two ways to have income: use your mind or use your back. You decide which is a better use of effort.

C) is the most powerful and ominous thing God left us when He made man in His Image. He gives man the freedom to choose. God cannot choose who you will be and what you will do. This is our choice. He doesn't fight our free will. You can be who you want to be. You can do what you want to do. You can believe what you want to believe. Everything is our hands. Your decision will determine your future.

Deuteronomy 11:26 – I am setting before you today a blessing and a curse.

It's your choice each day for blessings or curses. Everything is in front of you. You can do what you want to do and believe what you want to believe.

The Ideas we pursue comes from imagination. Without Ideas, as humans, we cannot make a change. This change comes because we get new Ideas. Always keep writing your Ideas down. Your mind receives new things and ideas which can change your life and bless the people around you.

2) Find the need

Dreamers are always are looking to meet needs and for ways how they can solve problems. People who are able to solve problems are dreamers. People who dream solve the needs of those who can't. Therefore dreamers get hired, get jobs and support. Dr. Mike Murdock said, "your next exit is the problem around you."

3) Prophecy

Many people receive a word from others and believe it, and it becomes reality. In the Bible, great people received the word from a prophet or from an angel. Soon they believed and it became reality. Any time someone speaks and it touches your spirit, you need to listen. That is your message. That message will change your life as you follow it. This time is your time! God will not send the Angel again. He does, however, send people to follow up and speak over your life.

Mary believed the message from the Angel Gabriel right then and the message became reality. Anyone who has dreams needs to learn from Mary; the mother of Jesus. We learn from Mary what is possible, that from the invisible comes the visible. Everyone has an assignment and you need to know it and to fulfill it. You are born to deliver something to this earth. Once you know it you can do it.

15 Things We Learn From Mary

1) Believe the message. Mary believed the message from the Angel. Even though it was a strange message, she believed what the angel said. Open your ears and brain to listen and

understand the entire message around you. You will find your message to the people when you listen.

> *Luke 1:38 – "I am the Lord's servant," Mary answered. "May your word to me be fulfilled?"*

Then the angel left her. Mary was having a reason not to believe the troubling message of the angel, but she chose to believe it even when it was not easy for her. You can believe what is in your mind. It will then be a reality.

2) Understand the dream in this message was from an angel from God! But that did not make it easy. Still, she needed to accept it. All around you, there are messages. Listen carefully. Your message may come from one of these people. Whether you like it is not the issue. It can still be a true message to change your life.

> *Luke 1:29 – Mary was greatly troubled at his words and wondered what kind of greeting this might be.*

3) You are born to deliver something to this world. God made you with purpose, therefore you are on the earth to fulfill God's plan. God will use you to fulfill his purpose that is why you exist on the earth. This is not an accident. You must ask yourself, "what is the plan of God for my life?" God used Mary to fulfill his plan. What will God do in your life? Could He use you to deliver a message, just like He did through Mary? Will you let Him?

For all the promises of God he usually uses a person to fulfill his promise. That is His favorite method. You are here on earth to fulfill the plan and the promise of God. God used Mary to fulfill his promise. You need to think about your life and ask what God will fulfill in through your life. Be available to be used by God.

Isaiah 9:6, for to us a child is born,
to us, a son is given,
and the government will be on his shoulders.
And he will be called
Wonderful Counselor, Mighty God,
Everlasting Father, and Prince of Peace.

4) Your Dream is a virgin. Mary didn't understand how it would happen. She had not been there yet. She had never heard anything like this from anyone else, but she believed. Your dream may be a virgin too. Of course, a new dream is virgin to you for you have never been there yet. You may dream something and no one you know is having this dream. But it's possible.

Luke 1:34 - "How will this be," Mary asked the angel,
"since I am a virgin?"

5) Your Dream will require God's involvement. In everything you are going to do God will be in you. Don't fear anything. You are going to do God's work so God will be with you. There are times you wonder what will happen. Fret nothing. God will be there for you.

Luke 1:35 - The angel answered, "The Holy Spirit
will come on you, and the power of the Highest will
overshadow you. So the holy one to be born will be called
the Son of God."

6) You will need the right people so that you are able to fulfill your dream. You need teachers and mentors that you can learn from them. After Mary conceived, she went to Elizabeth's house for friendship and more instruction. When you are with the right people your dream will keep moving.

> *Luke 1:39-41 - [39] At that time Mary got ready and hurried to a town in the hill country of Judea, [40] where she entered Zechariah's home and greeted Elizabeth.[41] When Elizabeth heard Mary's greeting, the baby leaped in her womb, and Elizabeth was filled with the Holy Spirit.*

7) You must act as soon as you realize your dream. You need to go where your dream will grow and be protected. Mary went to Elizabeth to receive new instruction, yes, but also protection. Your dream needs your action, your decision, and wise protection.

8) Move to the right environment, where people believe in you and support you. When you are pregnant you need the right people and more so a good place so your baby (the Good News you bring) will keep moving aright.

9) Your dream will impact the public. You will know you have the right dream because the right dream benefits others. If your dreams benefit only yourself, that is not a dream. That is your ambition; just your selfish desire. The purpose of your dream is to benefit others.

10) You must know the right location for your dream. Your dream requires a good location for God works in places. And He blesses you there so you can achieve your dream. Starting right anchors you for more.

11) Your dream has time and process. You need patience for the right time to come. On this earth, everything has a proper season, not just anytime - the right time. If your dream is big, you need to know that it will not happen overnight. Things that grow too fast tend to warp. It will take time, Relax. Your dream helps you mature. Take your time. It will come to pass.

Luke 1:56 – Mary stayed with Elizabeth for about three months and then returned home.

12) Your dream is hidden and perhaps unknown to what you are doing today. Behind what you are doing you will find your dream. It will benefit many people. That is how you will know this dream comes from God.

13) Many people will not accept your dream at the start. Don't give up, keep moving ahead. God will bring the people who will believe your dream and support your dream. When Mary delivered Jesus in Bethlehem no one believed her. She didn't get any support from anyone there. She labored among the farm animals. But God sent shepherds and wealthy wise men from the east. Their bringing of treasure supported Jesus' childhood.

Matthew 2:11–12 – On coming to the house, they saw the child with his mother Mary, and they bowed down and worshiped him. Then they opened their treasures and presented him with gifts of gold, frankincense, and myrrh. [12] And having been warned in a dream not to go back to Herod, they returned to their country by another route.

People who live with you may not see your greatness, but your star will be seen by people from far away. Some people may not believe your dreams or support you. But God will let people from far see you and support your dream, so just keep moving. They are on their way to you. Don't give up.

14) The Provision you receive is not for you, it's for the dream you have. The gold that the wise men brought was not for Mary, it was for her baby. Many people misuse the resources they receive. They think it is for them. That is wrong. Any resources you receive is for "the baby"; what you deliver.

Your 'baby' is the dream you are having now. Businesses fail and people fall because they use resources in the wrong ways. God supplies resources for making sure the dream keeps moving on.

If God trusts you with enough finances, that is provided for your vision. If you misuse your finances, in my opinion, it's like a person who has received authority from the government and then misuses it. Or a police officer whom the government trusts with authority and a gun but he uses it in a wrong way; on his own ambition like for revenge.

15) God will remove the enemy from your way so that you can keep moving. He will fight for you. Do not fear an enemy nor people who disagree with you. They will believe you when you reach your destination. So don't worry about a thing. Many people are suspicious and don't believe others. But as soon as you achieve your dream they will follow you.

4)   By Teachings

Any time your teacher is teaching you, you can decide to believe his teaching and you can become great if you believe his teaching. Anything you believe you can live it. And you need to live it according to what you now believe.

Romans 10:17 - So then faith comes by hearing and hearing the word of God.

Everything you learn you must believe it and put it in action. Then it can come true. No one will believe on your behalf. You must believe who you are, then put in action what you know, then persevere as you wait. The good times will come to pass. Twelve disciples learn from Jesus, Joshua learned from Moses, Ruth learned from Naomi, Elisha learned from Elijah. You can get the dreams verified through your teacher and believe his teaching yet only you can change your life.

5) Circumstances

Allow the challenges you are going through to motivate you. Think about how you can get the most out of the problems you are going through. These matters help you start dreaming about solutions.

6) Imitation

When you see other people doing what you feel in your heart is right and good, know that these things are possible for you too. Imitate them. Some dreams you are born with. Some become a reality to you when they are spoken by others. Everything we do isn't new. It has been done, as there is nothing new on this earth. If you don't know what to do, look at other people who do what you admire, you can start dreaming and be great like them.

CHAPTER 3

Passion

Passion is something that you are strongly interested in and enjoy doing. Anything you are passionate for is your career.

As a dreamer and a person who wants to archive his dream, the first thing that you need is to know and understand your passion very well. Keep focus on your passion. That will help you to achieve your dream easily since you are doing what you like.

4 Things you must do to achieve your dream

1) You must know your gift and know it well.

You need to know your talent, know what area you have been called to, and what you have been born to do. God has put inside you the talent which will help you to get where you want to go. Every human has his own talent and his uniqueness. You must know the distinction between you and others.

God is smart. He does not give you work without trials. You will get used to the work He will give you to do. Persevering through trials reveals your talent. Your talent will help you and make room for you in God's Kingdom.

> *Proverbs 18:16 – A gift opens the way and ushers the giver into the presence of the great.*

> *"If you do not know where you have come from, it's difficult to determine where you are. It's even more difficult to plan where you are going."*

> ~*Rev. Joseph Lowery*

2) You must develop your gift.

You must educate yourself to empower your gift. It is good to learn something you love. Many people go to school to just to learn and get a good job, but education must be the empowerment of your gift. Education will help you to be professional in your passion.

3) You must protect your gift.

Everything in life can be lost or stolen, so you need to protect yourself and your gift. Know well what you need to do and be aware of your limitations to protect yourself. The best policy is to be honest in everything you do and say. You can be talented, but if no one believes in your gift, it will not help you. Deviating from God's plan can lead you to abuse your life and your gift. You must be humble and respect others.

4) Exercise your gift.

You must start using your gift. If you have gift, but do not use it, it will not help you. No one will know who you are in relation to your gift. You need to show people who you are and what you have. If you do not do anything, it is like you do not have anything. The gift unused is like hidden gold. It does not have any value until it gets into the hands of someone.

Passion is the only thing that can help you to keep moving on even when things are not going right. Passion will keep you joyful when you do something you love to do. The day I had discovered my passion and my calling that is the day that joy came into my life. I find out that I love to pastor and motivate through speaker. I remember that in 2003 and since that day I have endless joy in my life. Even when things are not going well but I can believe that one day all will be right.

I have been ordained as senior pastor of The Refuge Church. Since 2009 I Pastor and do not receive a salary. I work multiple jobs to support my family while being full time pastor. For pastoring I am unpaid. And I love it anyway. I enjoy doing what I love to do, and in this I keep helping and supporting other refugees. I so enjoy doing what I do.

I needed a pastor for guidance even before I came to America. After I got my citizenship, I decided I would be going to the refugee camp to encourage my brothers who were still living the life I use to live. I went there every year. I went to Africa in 2019. I have had conference in Kenya. I went to Rwanda and in Uganda to the Nakivala refugee camp, When I got there, I saw how my brothers and sisters from Congo were living. I spent all the money I had. I was supposed to take a flight from Kampala to Nairobi then take my flight to US. But when I saw what was going on, I decided to take the bus so I could help them with my flight money. I helped them, then I took the bus from Uganda to Nairobi. When I was in Rwanda, I went with by bus then from Rwanda to Uganda and then Kenya, Nairobi. It is almost 1200 kilometers.

Then I took my flight from Nairobi to Chicago. My brother was supposed to come to pick me up. It was in the morning and he was at work. I went to the rental car desk, but then I cannot afford it. So, I took the bus. When I was in the bus, my supervisor called to tell me that I was on schedule to work that night. I tried to tell him how tired I was, but he told me that even though they had been covering my shift that now they cannot any longer. When we got to Lafayette, Indiana, the bus broke down. My nephew came to pick me up. Three hours later, I was at work. I asked myself, "Why I am doing this?" The answer was, "Passion makes me do this." I was happy and I felt so good. Everything was normal to me.

When you find that you keep complaining and are not feeling happy because you are doing something you do not like, try to make a connection with your passion. The promise of a good check should not be your main reason to work. Do it because you have passion for it.

I kept building my credit. In 2018, my wife and I had enough funds to buy land and then we built a five-bedroom house. I want to tell you that America is the country of opportunity for everyone. Do not discriminate yourself to the opportunity around you. Maybe you have met some people who told it is impossible to succeed in America. But to me, I believe everyone who wants to be successful in America can do it. It is possible because people born in America have a lot of opportunity. As an immigrant, I could not have chosen any job that I wanted, but I became successful with the job I could get.

Chapter 3: Passion

CHAPTER 4

Put Your Dream into Action

Everyone has a dream. A dream is a desire. It is about you to think about your future. But a great dream without being put into action is just thinking and you will never achieve anything. Your life is hidden in you. You will be who you think you are. No one will make you great. Other people will support your greatness, but they cannot dream for you or work for your dream. You are the one who will work for it.

Your dream belongs to you, but you will need others to be able to achieve your dream. Your friends and your relatives can help you to achieve your dream, but they cannot dream for you. Your boss can hire you, but he cannot work for you. If you need money from your boss, you need to work. If you are doing nothing, you will get nothing. If you have a dream and do nothing – if you keep talking about your dream and doing nothing, then that is the sign tell you that you will never achieve anything.

6 Things to help you to achieve your dream

1) You must clearly understand your dream.

As much as you clearly understand what you are going to do, it will give you greater confidence. Confidence helps you to be sure that you are going to achieve your dream. It will be easier for you to explain to other people about your dream. If you can't understand your dream very well, you are going to find it very hard to convince other people to help you. You will influence other people to flow your dream according to how you tell them. As much as you clearly understand your dream will influence how other people understand your dream.

You will never get to where you want to go if you don't know your destination before you start your journey. Your vision is like GPS. You must set up the destination before you start the journey. No airplane flies into the air before the pilot sets up the destination. If you fly without know your destination, you can get lost. Many people have good dreams but because they lack to define their dream. They keep changing their dream and then they lose it. You can lose your dream; you must keep your focus on your dreams as much you clearly understand your dream.

2) You must do what you plan to do.

It's very important to be a man of your word. Do what you say you are doing to do. No one will believe you if you keep changing your word. If you keep your plan flowing, you will achieve your dream. As you keep moving on, your progress may not be fast, but keep moving forward as Dr. Martin Luther King said:

> *If you can't fly, run. If you can't run, walk. If you can't walk, crawl. Whatever you do, keep moving forward.*

As you keep moving on, you are coming closer to achieve your dream. It was not easy when I started my journey. It was the only hope. I didn't have anything, but I didn't give up. I have received a lot of rejection, but I kept flowing with my passion and my dream. I have not yet gotten to where I am going, but I move on every day.

3) You must set up goals.

If you want to keep moving forward with your dream, you must set up your goals. If you set up your goals, it will help you to know your progress every day. To make sure you are running with your dream, you must have two things:

- Short-term goals

It will help you to know what you are going to do in a short period. It will help you to prioritize your time. Short-term goals help you with time management. That is only a good way to manage your time and to keep helping you to manage your success.

- Long-term goals

Long-term goals help you to focus on your future: what you need to do or what you will be in the future of your life. As you are planning long-term goals, you will have a clearer picture of where you will be. It will help you to keep having a focus on what you want to achieve in life.

Long-term goals determine your legacy, and what you need to tell other people about your future and that is your legacy you will leave behind.

4) You must believe in yourself.

You must believe that you are able to achieve the dream you have - that it is the plan of God in your life. God created you with the purpose, and no one will fulfill your purpose on your behalf. You are only the one who will fulfill the assignment that God has given to you. No one will do it for you.

Any dream you have is for you. You are the one who will make it come to pass. Many people will discourage you, but believe your dream is a part of your life. You will be remembered according to what you did not just what you said.

You are only the one who knows you more than other people. Other people can see you, but they don't feel you. Only you are the one who understands the dreams you are having. Don't let people turn you down. Don't accept the negative opinion of people. Continue to believe what you believe.

You must know that you will never change negatively contagious people. They don't change and they don't believe others. Negatively contagious people always criticize others. Believe yourself: keep moving forward even if some people don't believe you. If you believe in yourself, you will succeed.

It may take time but try hard to educate yourself. Gathering more information will give you more confidence. Lack of enough information will make you lose more confidence. If you know what you are doing, you don't need anyone's approval. The more you know, then you can keep moving on and achieve your dream without anyone's approval. If you don't have confidence in your dream, that means you don't believe what you are doing. Always gather information; learn more. Educate yourself every day. That is the best way to build confidence. Knowledge is the best key to your dream. As you are gathering all knowledge you can, you are building more confidence and getting closer to your dream.

5) Believe in your dream.

You are the one who understands your dream more than anyone. If anyone discourages you or criticizes your dream, do not be discouraged. People do not where you are going or where you have been. You have your own purpose and a different assignment from others. Do not think that all people and your friends will believe in your dream. Some friends will show you the reasons you cannot succeed and why you cannot achieve your dream. Do not spend more time with the people who do not believe in your dream. Dream killers are the enemy of your life and your dream. That is why Joseph's brothers did not support him. They were only looking for a way to kill his dream.

> Genesis 37:5-7 - *5 Joseph had a dream, and when he told it to his brothers, they hated him more. 6 He said to them, "Listen to this dream I had: 7 We were binding sheaves of grain out in the field when suddenly my sheaf rose and stood upright, while your sheaves gathered around mine and bowed down to it.*

You will never know your enemy until you have announced your dream. Sharing your dream is the best way to discover your enemy. As soon as your enemy knows your dream, he will come to fight you. His purpose is to kill your dream. Do not be afraid! You cannot defeat the enemy that you do not know. The first step to defeat the enemy is to know him. The sooner you find out, the better. There are people who you associate with that do not believe your dream. You must leave them as soon as you find out they are not supporting your dream. That is the sign to tell you that this is not the right place for your dream. Your dream is like a baby child. You must take care of your dream. Your dream requires ten things:

- Your total focus

- Your attention

- Your time

- Routing in your life

- Your protection

- Your care

- Protection

- Be ready to fight for your dream

- Pay the price required

- Be unique

Do not be discouraged with people who have already failed. There are many people who have had a great dream, but since other people told them they cannot succeed they believe them, and their dreams died. Just because other people do not believe does not mean you have to believe their opinion. *Do not change your theology and your philosophy to accommodate the situation.*

Keep believing in your dream. Sometimes your enemy will help you to move more quickly toward your destiny. The enemy can challenge you to work hard on your dream. Do not fear the enemy of your dream. You must work hard to prove them wrong. At the end of time, those people who discouraged you will one day respect you according to what they see.

You must have faith and believe you are already where you are going. If you see the picture about where you will be, you are already there by faith as Jesus said:

Mark 11:24 - Therefore I tell you, whatever you ask for in prayer, believe that you have received it, and it will be yours.

Faith is the must key for your dream. If you don't believe it, you will never get there. You must believe your future is bigger than today. Every day things change. You will never change until you dream about change. Your dream will save your life. Without your dream, you will die the same as you are today. No one will change your life. You are only the one who will dream about your future, and you must have enough faith that your tomorrow is bigger than today.

Hebrews 11:1 - Now faith is confidence in what we hope for and assurance about what we do not see. This is what the ancients were commended for. By faith, we understand that the universe was formed at God's command so that what is seen was not made out of what was visible.

Start acting like you are already achieved your dream. You are already there. Tell people about your dream. Have confidence in your dream. Tell other people about your dream as proof of faith. If you aren't able to tell others about your dream, that means you don't believe your dream. You still have a long journey to success.

Tell other people, even they do not believe it or support you. Always talking about your dream is how you will keep motivating your faith. The pursuit of a dream is to produce the hope of change.

The proof of the true dream is how much you believe it in your heart. That is how you will know that you will achieve it. Even God himself said that you cannot please him without faith.

> *Hebrews 11:6 – and without faith it is impossible to please God, because anyone who comes to Him must believe that He exists and that He rewards those who earnestly seek Him.*

6) You must involve other people in your dream

You must involve others in your dream. You cannot succeed alone. Other people know what you do not know, and sometimes other people can see what you don't see. Everyone who has achieved great things has allowed others to be involved in their dreams. When God gave a personal vision, He gave it to people who would help Him to fulfill the vision. God gave His servants good people for wisdom and advice. When God called Moses, He gave Aaron to help him. When Jesus started his ministry, He called twelve disciples to work with Him in His own ministry. When God gave Moses instructions to build the tabernacle, God gave him wise people who would help him to build the tabernacle.

> *Genesis 31:1 – Then the Lord spoke to Moses, saying: "See, I have called by name Bezalel the son of Uri, the son of Hur, of the tribe of Judah. And I have filled him with the Spirit of God, in wisdom, in understanding, in knowledge, and in all manner of workmanship, to design artistic works, to work in gold, in silver, in bronze, in*

cutting jewels for setting, in carving wood, and to work in all manner of workmanship.

You will always need someone: that is the way to grow. What you need someone can provide it. What you do not know, someone knows. That is why we have teachers, mentors, and coaches. That is why business people spend thousands of dollars looking at how they can find partners and how they can publish what they are doing. They are looking to get the attention of the people because they know that you cannot achieve your dream without others. You will always need someone to help you.

You need to know that there are people who are coming in your life to help you to achieve your dream. But not all the people who are coming into your life are coming to support your dream. Some people are dream killers. You need to identify and know what the intention of the people is who are coming into your life. Regarding your dream, you must make sure you always associate with the people who are coming to support you and make sure your dream comes true.

You must listen to those people who are coming to give you advice about your dream. However, not all the people who are coming to you are able to give you the right advice but some of the people are coming to support your dream. If you do not listen to them, they will leave you and you will lose them. Every dreamer should listen to good advisers. All great people have great advisers. You will never find any great leader who does not have good advisers. If you want to achieve your dream, you must have great advisers who can tell you the truth about yourself.

Many people like people who are telling them sweet words. Most of the time sweet words cannot help you to move on.

Sweet words just give you comfort but you will not affect change. You need people who will push you and spur you on to achieve your dream.

I remember me told my wife about my dream and what I wanted to achieve. My short-term goals were to provide for my family and my ministry. I was working two jobs, was also a full-time minister, and I needed to help my children with their homework. One of my long-term goals was to write a book. When my wife returned home from work each day, she would ask me, "What about your dream? Did you do anything today about your dream?" I told her that I needed to write my book even if it was one page a day or maybe one chapter per week. She pushed me to finish this book. It is good to allow others to be involved in your dream.

Chapter 4: Put Your Dream Into Action

CHAPTER 5

The Enemy of Your Dream

Your dream is what you desire to be in the future. You are not there yet, but by your faith, you are already there. People who do not have faith have their doubts about why you cannot achieve your dream. Sometimes they give you the reason why you cannot achieve your dreams. The enemy of your dream can be anyone, a friend or a relative. The brothers of King David were the first people who did not believe in him. Anyone who opposes you in public or in private is the enemy of your dream.

5 Ways to conquer the enemy of your dream

1) Identify the enemy of your dream.

Many people will come to you. You must know their motives. Why are they coming to you? It is good to observe why these people are coming into your life. Some people are coming for good - to help you and support your dream. When Joshua met with the angel, he asked him, "Where do you belong?" He asked him the question, "Do you belong to us or our enemies?"

Joshua 5:13 - Now when Joshua was near Jericho, he looked up and saw a man standing in front of him with a drawn sword in his hand. Joshua went up to him and asked, "Are you for us or for our enemies?"

It is good to know about the people you associate with: do they support your dream or not? If they are not supportive, that is the sign to exit from that group of people. Many people think that support is only just money. That is wrong - there are more ways to support than just money. When allowing people to gain access to your dream, first they must have a passion to support you for your dream to come true.

You need to choose friends wisely. You need to stay with the people who have the same passion as you. Choose friends who want to help you to achieve your dream. Find friends who are comfortable with your progress - those who are happy when you succeed. Some friends are not happy with your progress especially those friends who are not happy with your success. For some reason or another, they become jealous of your success. They can become your enemy quickly.

2) Do not spend time with dream killers.

Spend more time with people who are supporting your dream, not with people who are criticizing your dream. If you keep associating yourself with people who do not believe in your dream, they will keep telling you that you cannot succeed. As you continue listening to them, you will start believing them because that is what you hear. The Bible says faith comes from hearing.

Romans 10:17 ...consequently, faith comes from hearing the message, and the message is heard through the word about Christ.

People who do not have dreams of their own are challenged to believe in your dream. Stay with people who are having a concept of their own dream life. Look for people who are like-minded because they will understand you. Do not keep staying with people who do not understand you. They will pull you back. They may be your relative, but if they cannot understand your dream that disqualifies them from staying with you. Search alternate company to help you to thrive.

Some friends like spending time with you, but it is filled with chatting -spending time only talking. Hanging out with you is doing nothing to work toward your dream. Consider carefully if they are helping you with anything about your dream. Talk alone can kill dreams. Maybe your relatives or your best friends want to spend a lot of time with you, but their presence will kill your dream.

You will be like the people you spend more time with, that is why King David said, "Don't walk or sit with wicked people."

> Psalm 1:1 Blessed is the one
> who does not walk in step with the wicked
>   or stand in the way that sinners take
>   or sit in the company of mockers,
>   but whose delight is in the law of the Lord,
>   and who meditates on his law day and night.
> That person is like a tree planted by streams of water,
>   which yields its fruit in season and whose leaf does
>   not wither
> whatever they do prosper.

3) Do not believe the negative word of the enemy of your dream.

When you are pursuing your dream, you may meet some people who will discourage you and tell you that you cannot fulfill your dream. They may tell you negative things and point out your weaknesses. If you believe the negative words from other people who do not believe in your dream, that can really damage your dream in a big way. Consider what happened when King David said, "I can kill Goliath."

> *I Samuel 17:28 – When Eliab, David's oldest brother, heard him speaking with the men, he burned with anger at him and asked, "Why have you come down here? And with whom did you leave those few sheep in the wilderness? I know how conceited you are and how wicked your heart is; you came down only to watch the battle."*

David's brothers did not believe that he could fight, but David believed in himself. David knew who he was, and he spoke with confidence. He knew he could fight and kill Goliath. He recalled how he killed the lion. You are only the one who knows your background. Others do not know your past.

The enemy you conquered in your past gives you the confidence to conquer the enemies in your future. Others may not understand you. You must be ready to answer the question with confidence to anyone who would have doubts about your dream. That is how David answered Saul and those people who did not believe in him.

> *1 Samuel 17:34 – But David said to Saul, "Your servant has been keeping his father's sheep. When a lion or a bear*

*came and carried off a sheep from the flock, I went after
it, struck it, and rescued the sheep from its mouth. When
it turned on me, I seized it by its hair, struck it and killed
it. Your servant has killed both the lion and the bear; this
uncircumcised Philistine will be like one of them because
he has defied the armies of the living God. The Lord who
rescued me from the paw of the lion and the paw of the
bear will rescue me from the hand of this Philistine."*

Always be confident to answer any negative question. Do
not spend too much time explaining your ability, where you
get your confidence, or how you developed your talents. Do
not waste your time. They will not believe you even if you
spent a day explaining how you are able to achieve your
dream. Doubters will not believe it. That is why David knew
very well his brothers were not going to change. He did not
spend more time with them.

*1 Samuel 17:29-31 [29] "Now what have I done?" said,
David. "Can't I even speak?" [30] He then turned away to
someone else and brought up the same matter, and the
men answered him as before. [31] What David said was
overheard and reported to Saul, and Saul sent for him.*

I have met a lot of people who are telling me that America
is a very hard country. You cannot succeed if you do not speak
good English and you do not understand the system. But I
tell them, I know it is not easy, but it is possible! Quite often
other immigrants, who have been in America a long time, tell
the newcomers, "American life is very hard." But we should
not always compare our lives with the lives of others. Each
person has his own destiny.

4) Keep moving forward even when no one supports your dream.

Do not think every day that things will go right. Even if things are going wrong, you must be convinced in your heart that this is the right way to your success. Keep moving forward. People who are great today are the same people who kept moving even when they had more challenges, but they did not quit. If you fail during the pursuit of your dream, you will only gain more experience. Ultimate failure happens if you quit.

Things to help you to keep moving forward

- You must have a passion for your dream, more than anything. You cannot quit anything you love, even you do not have anyone to support you or to listen to you. But because this dream is what you love, you will keep moving on and keep loving it. Your dream is like your fiancé. If you fall in love with someone like a boyfriend or girlfriend or give birth to a beautiful child, your heart is full of love. You will keep constantly speaking about him or her when meeting with other people. They may not see the beauty you are seeing, but your heart is full of love always seeing great beauty. You do not care what others are saying: you keep moving on with your love.

You must be strong to keep your mind focusing on your dreams. Your mind does not have time to be distracted to think about other things. You will always need to think about your dream. Think of what you can do now, and how you can keep moving forward every day.

Keep talking about your dreams, even when you are not there yet because your mind and your heart is full of your dream. You do not have time to think and talk about other things. That is how you will know that you are serious about your dream.

- Always see yourself as a successful man in the future and not in the present. You must see you today as a great person in the future. Then your future is not further away. You are closer to achieving your dream. Motivate yourself by thinking about your greatness and soon you will achieve your dream. You will be motivated to work hard and wake up and run with your dream again even you were feeling hopeless. If you always see yourself as a successful person, then you will not be like those ten negative spies who went into Canaan and when they saw their enemies, they saw themselves as grasshoppers. How do you see yourself?

> Numbers 13:31 But the men who had gone with him said, "We can't attack those people! They're too strong for us!" 32 So they began to spread lies among the Israelites about the land they had explored. They said, "The land we explored is one that devours those who live there. All the people we saw there are very tall. 33 We saw the Nephilim there. (The descendants of Anak are Nephilim.) We felt as small as grasshoppers, and that's how we must have looked to them."

I do not like spending too much time thinking about my past or my background, because my life is full of bad memories. But when I remember how I feel after working hard, I create the feeling that is the best way to move forward.

With hard work, you can change your life, your family, and even your community. None of us can change the past but I believe we can change the future.

- Someone who always like achieving is not someone who will fail soon. Always be positive. Think about your greatness, your achievements, and how you will change your life and your family and the other people around you. If you can focus on the problems that you can solve, that will give you more energy to keep moving on even when things are not going right, Be like Joshua and Caleb! They believed in their future, even though they still had to fight. Even though the enemy was before their eyes, they could see their victory.

And they spoke about it and brought hope to the people of Israel.

> *Numbers 14:8 If the LORD is pleased with us, he will bring us into this land and give it to us. This is the land flowing with milk and honey! 9 Do not rebel against the LORD, and do not be afraid of the people of the land. We will devour them like bread. They have no protection, and the LORD is with us. So, don't be afraid of them."*

When I am tired of seeing how things are going wrong, I think about how my life has changed from the time when I was growing up. I am able to give my children a good life and make a positive impact in my community. That gives me more power to start dreaming big and keep moving on and pursuing the future which God has already planned for me.

5) Keep connecting yourself with the people who are supporting your dream.

You need to understand not all people will understand your dream, but you will meet many people who will understand and support your dream. If you have not met with people who can support you, it is your responsibility to connect yourself with right people who will support you.

You are only the one who can share your dream with others. No one else will share your dreams with others. Do not be discouraged with the rejection of people who do not believe in you. They cannot trust that you will achieve your dream. There are people coming into your life who will discourage you. But like a great dreamer, you should keep sharing your dream and keep connecting yourself with great people who can take you to your next step. Do not keep your dream a secret! Share your dream: because where you want to go, someone is already there. Find those people who are already achieving what you are dreaming to do. That is how you need to choose friends. Those friends can impact your life.

CHAPTER 6

Mentorship

A mentor is someone you can learn from - anyone who already been where you want to go. He can teach you via his experience. If you want to succeed and accelerate toward your dream, you need to find a mentor. Mentorship is a relationship between two people Mentorship is a relationship between two people

Who should be your mentor?

1) Your mentor is someone who knows what you do not know.

Your mentor knows more than you. To qualify your mentor, you need know what you need. That will help you to know who your mentor will be. It is good to learn by other methods, but you will not learn everything from a book. You will learn what you need to know.

Anyone who is successful in a different career from your path may not be the ideal mentor. Because if you have a different passion and a different career, it will more challenging to make progress. You need to find someone who knows what you love. Your interest will bring you together.

2) Someone who has already been where you want to go.

You cannot choose someone to mentor you because you love him or because he is older than you. He may have the same passion as you and know more about what you are dreaming to do and where you want to go, but, if he has not been there, and he has never achieved anything, how do you believe he can help you achieve your dream when he cannot help himself?

That is why before you become a teacher, you must graduate from school. When they want to hire you, they ask you to bring your diploma. Then you are qualified to be a teacher. You teach what you have been learning. When you are going to choose your mentor, choose someone who knows what you need.

3) Someone who wants you to be successful.

The goal of your mentor is to make sure you are successful in your dream. He is there in your life to correct the mistakes you make and give you correct advice. A mentor will connect you with the right people. He will adopt you as his child. You are his legacy. Your mentor has the right to ask you any question to make sure you are doing the right things that will help you to grow every day. Your mentor is not comfortable with your present; his focus is on your future.

4) Someone who will tell you the truth.

Your mentor will not tolerate your mistakes. He will correct you and tell you what you need to do so that you can be able to succeed. Your mentor is different from your teachers or your friends.

I have known teachers who do not care about the success of their students. Not all teacher's fall into this category.

- Typically, a friend is comfortable with your present. Your friend does not necessarily think about your success. Your friends focus on your friendship, not primarily on your success.

- Your mentor focuses on your success and helps you to succeed. Your success is the focus of your mentor.

- Your mentor will not laugh at you when you do anything wrong or when you tell him what you did wrong. He will listen to you and give you right advise - what you should do or what you can do to make things right.

5) Someone who does not take advantage on you.

You need to make sure that anyone who could be your mentor must be someone who has a passion to support others to be able to succeed. The wrong mentor will take you as his customer not as his protégé. Your mentor will support you, not just give you his time and listen to you. He will think how he can help you. Someone who just listens to you and does not offer advice is not your mentor but just a friend, A good mentor will listen to you and give you the answer you can't find anywhere. He is there for you to help you.

THE REASON FOR HAVING MENTORSHIP

1) A mentor can help you to accelerate toward your dream.

Your mentor will help you to make your dream clear and make sure everyone can understand your dream. He will help you to eliminate your weaknesses. Not everyone can tell you what your weaknesses are. Your weaknesses can prevent you from being successful. Your mentor will tell you what you are doing wrong and what you are doing right. Your mentor will tell you what you can do and what you cannot do because your mentor has more experience than you.

Take time to ask your mentor some questions. Anytime you need help you need to turn to your mentor. Any time you want to do something, and you do not know if it is correct, ask your mentor's advice. That is how you will be successful with your dream and make your mentor happy. Every parent wants to see his children succeed. The happiness of your mentor is to see you succeed.

2) Mentors have more experience than you.

Your mentor knows what you do not know. He has achieved things before you. You will learn from your mentor because he knows what you do not. You may be a great person, but if someone has what you need, you need to be humble to get what you need. When choosing your mentor, choose someone who has knowledge to give to you. Someone who has the experience you need, not because he is great person or because he has money. Many people choose a mentor based on incorrect criteria. Choose someone because of his experience and his kindness to you. Some people have family money but no experience. You need someone who can teach you and deposit new information into your mind. That is the best key you need from your mentor. Your mentor is not there to give you material things. Your mentor will correct your mistakes and give you correct guidance and cover your weakness and the mistakes you can make.

3) Your mentor has more connections than you.

Your mentor will know how you can connect with many people and the right ones. Because your mentor has been there before you, he is more connected than you. You need to ask some questions about how you can connect with the right people. Your mentor will help you to know how you can connect with other people such as attending conferences and other meetings where you can meet with other people. The greatest way to connect yourself with other new people is to attend different events. Learn how to introduce yourself to others. You need to have your own business card. You must have your website or your own blog. Find where you can put up information about yourself and about what you are dreaming to do. You will never get any help until people know about your existence and know what help you need.

4) Your mentor is your reference.

Nowadays it is very hard to trust someone you meet for the first time. Many people do not know what to do when it feels like there is no one you can trust, and when you ask for help there is no one who can help you. What you need to do is to build trust. You need to take time to build relationships with others and you need to find a mentor. If your mentor trusts you, he will be your reference. In all job applications, they ask for your references. You need to understand the important of your references.

I used to be sad, when I was doing things for my community because no one was supporting me. When I asked for help, I received a negative answer. I started asking myself, "What am I doing wrong?" I considered how I was talking and how I was asking for help. I realized that everything was good, but the only thing was no one knew me, and they were not able to trust me the first time. I needed to be patient and build trust so they could know who I am, what I am doing, and learn my dream. Then they will have more information to choose to support me. You need to have references, because anywhere you go, they will ask you for your references. Be ready to provide your references. That is how you can be successful with your dream.

5) Your mentor will correct your weaknesses.

When you want to be successful, you need to identify your weaknesses and find out how you can eliminate your weaknesses. You can change. Your mentor will tell you what your weaknesses are and teach you how you can change. You need to educate yourself. That is the way to make yourself wise. If you want to be wise, you must be ready to be corrected and accept the challenges. When wise people challenge you, you must listen and be ready to learn. That is why teachers give student tests after teaching them. When your mentor asks you any question, you must answer that question with your all knowledge according to what you understand with all respect. It may be not a good question to you, but it will help your teacher to know how he can help you to succeed with your dream.

6) Your mentor is not comfortable with your present.

Your friends are comfortable with your present, but your mentor is not comfortable with your present. He is focusing on your future. Many people are comfortable with their present life. That is why they do not have time to pursue anything.

- There are only two things that make people to not want to pursue anything. One is being comfortable with their current situation. If you cannot think of anything to improve your life that is proof that you are comfortable with the life you are living. You may not like it, but you are comfortable with it. Once you feel the desire to change your situation, you will start to search for a deliverer. No one will help you to change your situation. You are only the one who can change your situation. You will need to keep asking other people until you find someone who will listen to you.

- Many lazy people are not comfortable with the life they are living now. But because they are lazy, they do not want to do anything. They want someone who can give them free things. They keep waiting and thinking that maybe one day my life will change for the better. Unfortunately, if that is your motto, I can tell you that you are lying to yourself. Without your effort, nothing will happen. You will die the same person as you are now. Nothing will change until you change your mind set and put in action what you are dreaming.

HOW TO FIND THE RIGHT MENTOR

1) Someone you love to hear.

Any successful person you like to hear can be your mentor. A mentor is someone who has something he can teach others. You cannot choose a mentor who cannot give you his time. You must have a great connection with one another. A mentor must love his protégés. You may like for someone to be your mentor but if he does not have the heart to mentor anyone, don't force yourself to be the protégé of someone who doesn't like you. Find a mentor who has a passion for mentorship.

2) Anyone who wants you to succeed.

Your mentor will help you to succeed with your dream. Your mentor will be there for you. He will speak on your behalf; he will make you trustworthy in an arena of new people. When you are going to a new place, build good relationships with people. Ask your mentor to introduce you to new people. A good introduction is a way to accelerate your dream. I have been rejected many times because I have not had anyone who could introduce me. It took me many years to build good friendships with people who could trust me. It has taken me many years to find a mentor. Many people want to support your dream, but you need someone who will be on your side. Do not think you will succeed alone: that cannot happen. You need someone to support your dream - that is a good way to get where you are going.

3) Someone who has succeeded in their career.

You need to have mentor, someone who understands what you are doing. He must be someone who has the knowledge about what you are doing. Many people keep trying to do things on their own, but that way takes a long time to succeed. It is good to work with others and to learn from others as well. You must have one mentor or more than one mentor: that is the greatest way to succeed easily. Do not pick someone to be your mentor because he is your friend. A mentor must have enough skills to teach his protégés to succeed.

4) You can learn from your mentor even if he does not know you.

You do not need to know someone in order to be able to learn from him. You can find someone who has the information that can help you to achieve your dream. You need to start learning from him without asking who he is or where he comes from. What you need is the correct information that can help you to be successful.

When I was struggling with life, I read the book of Dr. Myles Munroe. His book changed my life and I started to follow him and read more books. I had dreamed of visiting him or attending one of his conferences, but sadly he died unexpectedly. Even though I have never seen him in person, I have learned many things from him. Through the written message of Dr. Myles, I had a new direction in my life.

I have some mentors that I have not met yet, but they have made an impact in my life. I have been following Dr. Mike Murdock. I had read his books and I had been dreaming to meet him. It took me years to meet him. I was so happy to finally attend one of his conferences after following him for over ten years. All these people are my mentors because they have what I need. I can learn from them. That is a great way to achieve your dream and make a difference in your life.

5) You do not need to spend many years with your mentor.

You need to know the people who have the information you need to be successful with your dream. You do not need to meet your mentor or spend more time with him. What you need is his knowledge. Buy his book and follow him on the internet. You will get his message. It is important that you get all the information you need from your mentor. Do not think because your mentor is not able to give you enough time that you cannot learn from him or he does not like you. You need to understand successful people are busy and hardworking. You are not the only one who needs him. He has other business he needs to take care of. Any time you get an opportunity to meet a wise person, ask the right questions with great integrity. You want to make sure to secure your chance for another appointment. If you act like a fool, you will not get a second chance to meet great people. Learn to take notes when you are in front of a wise man. Then when you get home you can keep on learning by yourself.

When you attend a conference, you will see some speakers and it may be a once in a lifetime opportunity. But afterward you can continue to learn more things and change your life. Listen carefully and take notes and be ready to learn every time. That is a great way you can change yourself and make an impact in your life.

Chapter 6: Mentorship

CHAPTER 7

You Are Not Alone

When God gives you a dream, He even prepares the people who will be supporting your dream. You need to discover where these people are and how to find them. You must make your vision clear. That is why businesspeople hire business planners. You must know people who have same passion you. Find the people who understand your passion. You must tell other people about your dream. That is how you will find other people who have the same passion as you.

When God gives you a dream, He always prepares a door for you. One that can help your dream to thrive. Do not limit yourself. God can make a door for you anywhere. Be ready to share your dream and tell others where you are and where you are going. Some people will laugh at you, but the right people will support you and support your dream.

Every big dream starts small. Do not think that because your dream is small it cannot be great. Your dream can be great if you think it is possible. When things start going wrong, many people become disappointed and then they give up on their dream. Do not think everything is going to be fine every day. But when things are not going well, I want to remind you that Jesus said, "I will be with you always until the end of the age." In Matthew 28:20, God said, "I will never leave you or forsake you."

> *Deuteronomy 31:6 – Be strong and courageous. Do not be afraid or terrified because of them, for the Lord your God goes with you; he will never leave you nor forsake you."*

7 WAYS YOU CAN NOT FEEL ALONE

1) Let your family and relatives be involved in your dream.

When you have dream, you need to let your family know what you are going to do. They will tell you the truth about it and they will help you to achieve your dream. If you are married, you need to tell your spouse. He or she will be the first one to support you. According to the Bible, your spouse is your help.

> *Geneses 2:18 – The Lord God said, "It is not good for the man to be alone. I will make a helper suitable for him."*

I remember when I met my fiancé who is my wife today. The first thing I told her was my vision. I asked her if she felt comfortable to marry me. She needed to know who I was and what I want to achieve. She has been a great helper for my dream. She supports me in everything I am doing. She takes time to pray for me and uses her finances for our dream. As soon as we married, my dream became our dream together.

Maybe your spouse may not see things exactly as you see it, but because you love one another, you will support each other. You need to share your dream with your children. They are the first resource God has given to you. Your children need to understand your dream well. Take time to explain what you are dreaming and how they can support you.

I have four children. They are very young, but they know my vision. I take time and tell them about my dreams. I tell them my dream and how they will help me even if they cannot help me much today. But I believe in the future they will be able to help me if they understand my dream and like it. Children are a blessing from God.

Psalm 127:3 Children are a gift from the Lord; they are a reward from him.

Tell your parents what you are dreaming. They can be a part of your dream and will support you. Before you go out to start a home, tell your siblings your dream. They may not agree with you, but they must know your dream before anyone since these people are your blood. They love and they care about you more than anyone.

After Joseph had his dream, before he told anyone else, he told his brothers his dream. They disagreed with him and they planned to kill him, but he trusted them. It is good to start with your family first. Many people who are very successful in business are involved in a family business.

2) Share your dream with your friends.

Share your dream with good friends who can understand you and support you. God has given you good friends as a great blessing. Friendship starts with communication and great things. Friends are closer to you, who understand you and enjoy your friendship. Friends are good people to share your dreams with because they understand you and enjoy spending time with you. That is how you can have more people involved with your dream and that is how you will be able to excel in your dream. You will not feel alone when you are with your friends.

3) Ask other people to be involved in your dream.

You will not succeed alone. You need other people to be involved with your dream. Since God has given you a dream, you need God Himself to be involved and you need other people to support your dream. You will always need other people to help and to teach you. That is the greatest way to thrive. In life, many people like to do things alone, but they may take longer to keep moving forward.

You will need someone to go to the next level. Do not think you can achieve anything on your own. You may try to keep moving on, but you always need other people to achieve any success:

> *Ecclesiastes 4:9-12 two are better than one,*
> *because they have a good return for their labor:*
> *¹⁰ If either of them falls down,*
> *one can help the other up*
> *But pity anyone who falls*
> *and has no one to help them up.*
> *¹¹ Also, if two lie down together, they will keep warm.*
> *But how can one keep warm alone?*
> *¹² Though one may be overpowered,*
> *two can defend themselves.*
> *A cord of three strands is not quickly broken.*

4) Keep connecting yourself with the right people.

All friends are not the right people to support your dream. You need the right people to support your dream. Wrong people are the people who disagree with your dream. Right people are the people who support your dream. Right people will be comfortable with your weaknesses. Right people will be comfortable sharing great ideas with you and support you. Keep looking for the right people who are good to you and understand you and support your dream. If you want to progress with your dream, do not fear everyone. Many people do not trust anyone. Yes, some people are not good at supporting others. But imagine all the people who are the right people who can help you to achieve your dream.

Learn from the right people. Any time you meet with someone who knows more than you do, that the time to learn. Not all learning takes place in a classroom. Do not wait in school if you have passion to achieve something that can be accomplished outside of the classroom. The door to the knowledge you need for our dream could be anywhere. Walk through that door and invest your time there.

5) Visit other successful people and learn from them.

You must know other people who have succeeded before you. Identify some people who have succeeded in the same career. You need to visit them and talk to them. That is how you will gather experience and learn from others. Do not sit at home alone with your dream. Get out there and meet successful people. You must know people so you can learn from them. When the Queen of Sheba heard about the wisdom of King Solomon, she went to visit him in I Kings 10:1.

6) Attend more conferences.

It is good to educate yourself every day. That is the greatest way to gather more knowledge. Without knowledge you cannot progress. The way you can gather more information is to join other people who have enough knowledge to help you to succeed with your dream.

Many people do not understand the important of attending more conferences. At a conference, you will learn more knowledge and gather information and learn from others. You will meet more people who are very successful in different careers and then you can connect yourself with other people. Conferences are the greatest way to meet other people. That will help you not to feel alone and you will keep moving on with your dream. Attending a conference is a good way to meet the right people which is how God will help you gather greater knowledge.

> *Ecclesiastes 2:26 To the person who pleases him, God gives wisdom, knowledge, and happiness, but to the sinner he gives the task of gathering and storing up wealth to hand it over to the one who pleases God. This too is meaningless, a chasing after the wind.*

Successful people pay money to attend conferences. Poor people may think that conferences are a waste of money if they must pay to attend any conference. That is a poverty mentality. If you cannot pay for your own empowerment, you will stay the same and you will never progress with your dream.

7) Keep sharing your dream with the right people.

To succeed with your dream is not easy. Some time is required to succeed with your dream. It is not easy. You may need to keep trying many times. Keep busy sharing your dream with many people. Maybe one day, you will meet with some people who have the same passion as you or people who have compassion for you. They will support you in order to achieve your dream. Do not give up when some people do not believe in you. Keep approaching different people. You will make it. Just keep trying until you make it.

Ecclesiastes 11:6 - Sow your seed in the morning,
and at evening let your hands not be idle,
for you do not know which will succeed,
whether this or that,
or whether both will do equally well.

When I moved to America, I did not have anything - just a dream and hope. I was living in east Moline, Illinois, then I decide to move to Indianapolis to chase my dream. I did not know anyone, but I trusted God's favor. I started knocking on the doors of different churches and told people about my dream. I did not have enough time to share with a lot of people because I was spending time working and taking care of my children. I remember I went to meet some people. I took my children because I did not have babysitter and I did not have money to pay a babysitter. But I did not miss my appointment. I took my children to meet the new people. I think they understood and supported my dream. My passion was big then. It was to start a church and to keep supporting my community and to make sure they kept worshiping as they used to back home.

I kept knocking on different doors. One day I knocked on the door of Crooked Creek Baptist Church. I met Pastor Tom, who was the pastor at that time. He opened the door for us. We used the building. They gave me an office too. Now we keep growing as we keep working together and have

Board of Crooked Creek Baptist Church

joined the greater community. The board of Crooked Creek supported us in different ways.

Crooked Creek Baptist Church members have been supporting me since July 2013. We have been using this building free of charge for almost seven years. They pray for me when I go on mission. It has been a great blessing to work closer with people who love us and support us. We use the building every Sunday and for conferences. It was a great blessing to me and the Congolese refugees and all the central African community. We meet in this building as a community.

Many of the Congolese community of Rwanda and Burundi are looking for community when they get here to the United States. They work hard every day. We do not have time to meet on weekdays or hang out together otherwise. This is the only place we can meet and share information and socialize. We have time to have Bible study and personal prayers. I really appreciate what Crooked Creek Baptist Church has done for us.

Reader do not quit! Keep moving and share your dream with other people. One day you will meet with the right people.

Reverend Joan Friesen

I have been working under the American Baptist Church of Great Indianapolis (ABCGI). Rev. Joan Friesen leads ABCGI. She has been a great blessing to our ministry. She has supported me so much and she has been giving me much encouragement throughout these long years. She is such a wonderful woman of God. I have met a lot of great friends who have a great heart to support me and they take time to give me advice and say prayers for me.

Chapter 7: You Are Not Alone

CHAPTER 8

Principles

If you want to succeed, you must understand there are principles in this life. In this world, everything is about principles. You cannot change things, but you can follow the principles, and then you will succeed. If you want to enter heaven, you must follow the principles of God and if you want to succeed, you must follow the principles of successful people.

On this earth, God has made everything with principles. If you do not follow those principles, you will never achieve heaven. Everything you see on the earth has protocol to follow from humans to the animals and even to the trees. If you do not follow protocol, then nothing with happen. That is how God works. If you need anything you must ask yourself which principles, I need to follow to be able to succeed.

GOD MADE EVERYTHING WITH PRINCIPLES TO BE PRODUCTIVE

• A human being is to be productive. As men and women come together, they can have children. You may be a good-looking guy or lady, but you cannot have a child until another person comes into your life. That is God's principle.

• You may have good seed, but your seed cannot bear any fruit until you put it in the ground in good soil. Every seed needs to be planted somewhere. Without being planted, you will never harvest anything.

• If you need knowledge, you need to learn. You will never know something until you learn. It is not possible to be smart and have good knowledge without learning. You must take time for searching out knowledge: that is what the Bible tells us. You must seek knowledge about how you will be wise. Without a pursuit, you will not get anything. That is the principle of everything on the earth.

Proverbs 15:14 – The discerning heart seeks knowledge but the mouth of a fool feeds on folly.

• God has given the principle of time to everything on the earth. You cannot change God's time - days, months, and years. A woman delivers a child nine months after conception. The time of gestation is different for animals. Every animal has a different time to be productive.

• Everything grows by its time. You cannot change the time. If you plant any seed in the ground, you must wait for the right time before you will have a harvest. That is how everything works.

• When it comes to your dream, you must follow the principles of success. You must work hard for your dream. Nothing will come to you without your pursuit.

• You must share your dream with others, even if some of them do not believe in you. But keep speaking about your dream: that is one of the principles to move forward with your dream.

• The principle of production is inside every seed. You need only to obey the principles of the seed.

• Many Christians have a misguide understanding regarding spending too much time praying for success for their dream. Prayer is good, but you need to work hard for your dream.

• Prayer will help you to have a good relationship with God. But prayers alone will not help you to achieve your dream. You need to work for your dream. As the Bible tell us, you will enjoy the meal from your labor.

> *Ecclesiastes 3:13 – and also that every man should eat and drink, and enjoy the good of all his labor, it is the gift of God.*

• When you want to succeed, you must follow the laws and principles of success. If you don't follow the protocol of success and you try to use only your thinking, it is like to putting juice in a car. Then you think you will get where you are going running your car on juice. You will not get anywhere because the principle of the car is to put gas in it. Then it will move and take you anywhere you want.

• Jesus has given us three great principles of success. Anything you need, you must work for it. Consider these three principles:

- Ask: No one you will know what you need until you ask.

- Seek: You need to seek and what you need you will find.

- Knock: You must keep knocking on different doors. One day a door will open.

Matthew 7:7 – Ask and it will be given to you; seek and you will find; knock and the door will be opened to you.

• There is an easy way to prove that you are using the wrong principles regarding your dream: nothing changes. You stay in the same place and you achieve nothing.

• For everything you want to do, you have been given the tools you will use to be successful. You need to make sure you are using the right principles that will help you to succeed.

- Businesspeople use marketing to market their product and all businesspeople have two principles.

- A businessperson hires employees who will help them to achieve their goals.

- Politicians use campaigns. They take their time to tell people about their plan and how they will work for them.

- Churches are used to bring the congregation together. You can't campaign in the church. That would be the wrong tool. Always make sure you are using the right tools for everything you want to do.

6 PRINCIPLES OF SUCCESS YOU MUST FOLLOW

1) Follow the steps of success.

You must follow the steps of success. Do not think you will be successful overnight. The journey of success is like the life of human being. You cannot be a child and an adult in the same day. Your journey to being a great man is step by step. If you want to rush towards success as quickly as possible, you could commit a lot of mistakes. That is why many people are in prison. They decide to rob a bank so they can have the money they want quickly and without working. Many of them end up in jail. You need to follow the principles of success. Teach yourself to work hard. All successful people have rules to follow in their life.

- Successful people work hard.

- Successful people use their time wisely.

- Successful people spend money wisely.

- Successful people go to bed early and wake up early.

- Successful people build connections with important people.

- Successful people do not waste their time.

- Successful people do what is important for their dream.

Do not think successful people achieved their dreams by luck. It was not only by favor, they worked for it. They have spent day and night working for their dream. If you want to be successful, follow the steps of success. If you cannot, don't keep complaining and blaming others. You are responsible for your life. You will be what you want to be. No one will prevent you from doing what you want to do. It is your choice.

2) Follow the protocol of success.

Anywhere you go, you must follow protocol. If you attend any meeting, do not speak until you have been given the time to speak. Or ask permission to speak. If you are a speaker or a guest, ask how long you can speak or how long your meeting will take. It is good to be professional.

Any time you are with great people, you must follow protocol. If you cannot follow protocol, they will ask to you will never be invited. If you want to be successful, follow the protocol and ask about anything you do not understand. Many people feel ashamed to ask questions, but that is an easy way to educate yourself. If you are with great people, always make sure you are following protocol. If you do not follow protocol, you could lose an opportunity.

Proverbs 23:2 – and put a knife to your throat if you are given to gluttony.

If you are attending any event, you must follow the protocol of the event planner. This is the one key for your acceptance, and they may invite you back.

3) Follow the law of success.

Many people do not understand the power of the law and importance of the law. In life everything has been given laws as guidance. Every law has a punishment for disobedience and a reward for obedience. The Bible is a book of laws and principles and explains what will happen if you obey the law and what will happen if you do not obey the law. All countries have a law of guidance. If you do not follow the law, there is a punishment. Many people in jail are there because they wanted to be successful using a short cut. They do not want to follow the law and principles of success.

Many people who want to be successful in a short time, they die without achieving their dream. When they needed money, they robbed banks. They start fighting with the police and the security officers of the bank. Some die and end up in prison. Work hard for your dream. That is a great way to be successful. An easy way to be successful is to work smart. Connect with smart people who can teach and support you regarding your dream.

4) Follow the law of honor.

You must honor other people. Many people have great dreams, but they don't understand the law of honor. When you are around great people, learn how you can prove that you honor them. That will make them happy and they will think about how they can help you to succeed. No one can help arrogant people. Always be humble and honor those who are greater than you. You will not be great if you can't honor great people. Successful people honor each other. Treat each other with respect. Employers honor their employees. That is one of the keys to making them successful. Learn how to honor other people. If you can't honor others, it will be hard to succeed with your dream.

Learn how to honor your leaders. Wherever you are, you will work under leaders. You will work under a supervisor or under a manager. If you don't honor your employer, you will lose your employment, or you will never get promoted. Everyone on the earth wants to be treated with honor and respect.

5) Follow the principle of working hard.

Nothing will happen until you do something. Many people think they will be successful by luck. Then they keep waiting until they die without achieving anything. You must work for everything you want. Do not think someone will work for you. You are only one who will work for you. Because some people are very lazy, they keep thinking they will be successful tomorrow. They keep waiting and talking about success, but they are doing nothing. That means you are just thinking about success, but you will never be successful until you start working for your dream. Some Christians think that as they pray for their dream, that God will help them to be successful.

Since I was a child, my mother, who was a prayerful woman, served God as much she could. And she was a pastor who prayed, but our lives did not change. We did not know the principles of success. Prayer can help you to connect with God, but prayer is not the only answer to your poverty. You need to pray, but you cannot stop working because you are praying.

After I understood the principles of success, I started working. Even as I was praying, I worked hard every day. I worked more than one job, so I was able to provide for my family. Do not keep waiting. Stand up and go to work for your dream. Do not think you will be successful without working - that cannot happen. If you think you will be successful without working, that means you do not want any change in your life. For everything you want on this earth, you will work for it.

We have people who are waiting for other people to work for them. They keep asking for help or waiting for a parent or any relative to die so they can get an inheritance. Unfortunately, that is why some children kill their parents, do not think that someone will work for you. God promised Israel the Promised Land, but they had to fight for it. You need to pursue everything you want.

We have other people who do not work but they think one day they will be lucky and have everything they want. That is why they keep gambling. They think that they will win the lottery and be rich overnight. And they keep spending the little they have as they keep trying their luck by taking chances. That does not work for anyone who wants to be successful. Work hard for your dream.

Chapter 8: Principles

CHAPTER 9

Make a Difference

Thing may not be going as you want them to, but I write this book to tell you that it is possible to make a difference and change your life. You may have a bad background. But as long as you are still living, you are able to make a difference and move beyond your background. Some people keep living with their past life. You should let your past go. If you keep holding onto your past, you will never move to the next level. You must focus on your future and not focus on your past.

We learn through the mistakes we make. But if we do not focus on our future, our past will control our thinking and we cannot move on and make a difference. I do not think much about my background. I spend more time thinking about what I can do in the future but not about my past. I have decided to make a difference even though it is hard. It is impossible to change my background, but I always tell myself that I will never allow my past to affect my future. I can make a difference in my life, in my family, and even in my community. I believe God and I believe His Word. The Bible tell us that anyone who is in Christ is a new person. The old things are died because we are new in Jesus Christ.

> *2 Corinthians 5:16-17 - so from now on we regard no one from a worldly point of view. Though we once regarded Christ in this way, we do so no longer. Therefore, if anyone is in Christ, the new creation has come:] The old has gone, the new is here!*

25 WAYS YOU CAN MAKE A DIFFERENCE

1) Think like a victor not like a victim.

Everyone has a background, good or bad, but it may affect how you are thinking about your future. Problems are not permanent. You are in a passing situation. Do not think that the situation is permanent. You may go through a lot of problems, but do not think like a failure, think like a victor. Jesus said we are more than conquerors.

> *Romans 8:37 - No, in all these things we are more than conquerors through him who loved us.*

Everything will depend on how you choose to believe. You must believe in your victory and not see yourself as a failure. Judas Iscariot and the Apostle Peter had a similar problem in that they didn't always agree with Jesus, but Judas decided to kill himself. Peter repented and became a preacher: how do you see yourself? Even if you are a victim, choose to see yourself as a victor. You are the only one who will change your situation. Sometimes you will feel that no one cares about you. You must take care yourself. Change your thinking.

If you keep thinking like a victim, you cannot help others if you cannot help yourself. As a person, you want to make a difference. Forget about your failures and your challenges. See yourself as a person who will make an impact in your country as a person of values.

I have been victim to different things in my life, but I do not spend any time seeing myself as a victim. I see myself as a successful man, who works hard every day to keep moving on. I believe in my dream and one day I will live the life I am dreaming about. I do not worry about how many challenges that I will face in the future. I must be a person who keeps my focus on my dreams.

2) Your mess is your message.

Sometimes people say that they do not have a message they can give to others or how they can encourage those people who are going through different challenges. Your mess is your message. Think of the problems you have been through. Share how you went through that situation. Change your mess to your message. Do not feel ashamed to share with others what you have experienced. That is the message you have, and you know it very well because it is your own experience. That is your authentic message because you are speaking according to your experience. Do not that you will make a difference only after having a master's degree. Just share from your own experience and you will make a difference.

3) Think how you can make an impact on others.

When you want to make a difference, think how you can make an impact on others. Do not keep focusing on your problems. Think how you can be blessing to others. Everything you do for others; God will do for you.

Ephesians 6:8 – Knowing that whatever good anyone does, this he will receive back from the Lord, whether he is a slave or free.

You need to care for others, who…

4) Accept who you are.

Do not be ashamed to share who you are and what you have been going through. That is a part of you, and you cannot change your background. You are who you are, and no one can change who you are. It does not matter what you have been going through. You are unique and stronger for it. Because of it, you can make a difference with your life.

Do not imitate other people. Be who you are and be strong. Keep focusing on your own "strongness." You may have some weakness, but you still have your own strengths which amount to more than what others may have. Many people on this earth need your help throughout your life. Do not think you are useless because of what you have been going through. You are a strong vessel of God. He will use you in a mighty way if you are ready to be used. Do not ignore yourself. You can make a difference and make an impact just as you are.

Tell other people what you can do and what you cannot do. Tell them about your challenges and the way that is required to move forward. Accept who you are, and you will get the help you need.

5) Do not quit.

Do not quit because things are not going according to how you want. Keep moving on and keep trying until you achieve what you want. If everything goes wrong one day, it does not mean that every day will be the same. Be a person of perseverance. Keep doing what you have been called to do.

Failing once is not failure. Quitting is failure.

On this earth, you have an area to which you have been called. You have something you have been born to do. No one will do it until you have it. Keep following your passion. Do not quit. One day you will achieve your dream and you will make a difference. There is something you can do that no one can do.

Do not quit what you are doing and follow others because they are doing it better. Keep doing what you have been called to do. Some day you will be excellent in what you are doing as you are keep focusing on your passion.

6) See yourself as a successful person.

In your mind always think like a person who has been successful. Everything will depend on how you see yourself. It does not matter what you are going through in your life. See yourself as a winner. Every word you speak, everything sounds like everything in the universe. If you see yourself as a failure, you will fail. If you see yourself as a successful person, you will be successful and make a difference in your life and even make an impact on others.

7) Always think about how you can help others.

In everything you do, think how you can be a blessing to others. That is how you can make a difference in other people's lives. Do not live a selfish life. Always find people who have problems around you and help them. That is the way to live a great fulfilling life. What you are doing for others, God will make happen for you.

Great people always keep helping others. That is the way to give back in your community and even to God who have given to you what you already have. You can't give back to

God directly, but you can give to His people. That way you can make a difference with your life.

8) Accept your difference.

You need to know that you are you - unique and different from others. Do not think that you need to be like someone who is successful. You are who you are. You are different. Do not imitate others. Find who you are then do everything as you. Find your difference from others. Find your passion in your heart and then do what you are feel you should do from your heart.

You cannot be like others, but you can do what you feel you can do. You can do what other people do, but you can do it in your own unique way. Many people try to be like others, but always be you. Do not despise your gift. Everyone has his gift and his greatness inside him. It does not matter what you have been going through - your gift is still inside you. Even if you are a victim, you can still use your gift and make a difference.

As a person who has been a victim in different situations, I accept who I am although I choose not to accept a bad situation that I have been going through: a situation that might threaten to take away my passion and my gift. Even though I do not have enough support, I still believe that I am who I am, and I can make a difference and change my life for the better.

9) Leave your comfort zone.

Some people think that they will only be successful if they keep working with the people, they know such as people from their community or from their own culture. You need to go beyond your comfort zone. Learn from different people.

That is the way you can learn new things and take yourself to a different level of your dream. As people we can become comfortable and live life as we have been used to, but if you want to be successful, do something you have never done before.

We like to keep our own culture, but you can learn more through others. Make a point to try new things. That is the way you can succeed, and you can make a difference by learning different things from others.

10) Dream big.

Do not limit yourself. Dream big as much as you can. God has given us everything we want, but as human beings we limit ourselves with fear. Sometimes we limit ourselves by thinking of small dreams. God has given us a great brain with a capacity for thinking big and dreaming big things, but we may be scared to dream big. The whole world belongs to you. Do not limit yourself. Everything you can imagine in your mind; you are able to do it.

Do what you have a passion for. You can do it. Do not fear – just go for it. Do not be afraid regarding your dream. You cannot make a difference without a big dream. It does not matter if many people will not believe in your dream. As you believe your dream, you will achieve it. Does not worry about failing. Keep dreaming big.

God has already given you everything you need, but people limit themselves in their mind with negative thoughts. You must think big about your life. Dreamers change the world. Dreamers give jobs to those who do not dream.

Without dreaming, you cannot make a difference. You need to think about how you can make a difference in your life. Dreamers make the world better.

11) Keep trying.

Do not give up. If you fail, it does not mean you are done. You need to tell yourself that you are not done yet. Failing mean two things:

1) You still need experience.

2) You still have a long journey to your destiny.

If you want to make a difference, do not quit. Keep trying until you achieve your dream. It is important to keep trying - that is the proof of your focus. To keep trying is the proof of your faith about your dream.

12) Keep asking.

Do not be ashamed to ask anyone for the help you need. There is no one on this earth who knows everything. For whatever you do not know, there exists someone who does know. If you ask for help, do not think you are stupid, or you are embarrassing yourself. It is a normal life activity to ask for things.

Always ask so you will know what you do not. Without asking you will never know what you do not know.

Asking questions is the best key to gathering knowledge. Children are not ashamed to ask any question. That is how they will know more things is because they are not afraid to ask questions. Do not stop asking questions. That is the key that will help you to open many doors.

People will know what you need as soon you ask for help. Others will help you if you ask for any help; you will receive what you have asked. What you need is what you should ask for.

Asking questions is not stupid. It is the way to know what you do not know.

13) Search for opportunities.

You need to search for opportunities around you. As you are going from place to place, keep thinking and looking for what you want. If you see anywhere that you can do something, do it. Do not think opportunities will come to you. You are the one who will go to where you can find opportunities. Many people think that opportunities will come to them without pursuit. That cannot happen. You are the one who needs to be looking for where you can find opportunities.

You will find opportunities by meeting new people and attending conferences. Keep going where you can meet successful people who know what you do not know; people who have been where you have never been yet. Find people who have already achieved what you are pursuing. Whatever you need, someone will have it; it is your responsibility to go where you can find an opportunity.

14) Find greatness in you.

You need to know your gift. Your gift makes you unique. Your gift will open doors for you and make you great. Many people are so blessed with different gifts, but they don't use them. Your gift makes you different. Everyone has a gift. God has blessed everyone with a gift which will make him great.

Proverbs 18:16 – A man's gift makes room for him, and bringeth him before great men.

Find your talent - you will be great by using your talents. Do not keep trying to imitate others. You will waste your time by trying to be like someone else. Be you. Think about how you can do something great. Consider what you have been going through or how you are the image of God. God believes in you. You can change your life and helping others if you can believe that. Sometimes we think we need help and we keep focusing on getting help from the outside but if you want to have long-term help, think how you can help yourself. Find out your greatness - how you can solve your own problems. Do not give up. Do not dwell on the worries of life. Do not kill yourself. Do not live with a life full of stress. Stop crying. Think as a great person on how you can solve your problems in your life.

I have lived a life full of problems and sorrow. I could find no one to help me. If I cannot help myself, no one else will change my life. If I cannot change my life, I started to ask myself about what I can do and about what I am able to do. What I cannot do, I ask for help. I started connecting myself with the right people. I did not know anyone who could help. Some people rejected me. Other people welcomed me with great joy. Now I am who I am because of searching how I could help myself to change my thinking in a positive way.

15) Change your social circle.

If you want to change your life, think about how you can change your circle of friends. You will be like the people you spend time with. You will believe what you see and what you hear. If all your friends are only talking about their problems and how their life is very hard, your life will be hard also.

Associate yourself with successful people who are talking positively about life. That will help you to believe that you can achieve something too.

Some people stay in their own problems because in their social circle no one can solve their problem. But if you have great friends who can solve any problem, they will help you. But many people relate to other people who have some challenges. If you are poor, it is not easy to connect with successful people. But try to find even one person who can listen to you. He will teach you to go where you want to go.

If you want to be great person who can do something you have never done, leave your social circle and build new friendships with those who can teach you what you do not know.

I moved to Indianapolis. I left all my friends and members of my family in Rock Island, IL. I did not know how I would survive by myself, but one of my goals was to have new friends and keep moving on with my dreams. I visited many churches and I went into restaurants. I was looking for someone to greet me and ask me any question. Or I greeted them and asked questions about them. I have many friends now. You must think about how you can change your life because you are the one who knows what you are going through.

16) Find a role model for yourself.

You need to know the people who inspire you; the people who you want to be like. Certain things in life are learned by imitation. You need to learn from others. You will never do something new. Everything is already done. You need to learn from those who are already successful in their dream.

You must find the people who inspire and motivate you. Those people may have more information that you need to able to succeed with your dream.

There are people who have inspired me. I started following their messages every day and reading their books. I spent more money buying books. The first time I bought a book was when I was motivated by one of my role models. When I read the book, the role model became my mentor.

You need to learn how you can gather information together. That is the way you can succeed.

17) Refuse to fear.

Fear is the greatest enemy that will prevent you from succeeding. You need to remove fear from your dream. You cannot move forward if you still are afraid in your mind.

> *Romans 8:15-16 - [15] The Spirit you received does not make you slaves, so that you live in fear again; rather, the Spirit you received brought about your adoption to sonship. And by him we cry, "Abba, Father." [16] The Spirit himself testifies with our spirit that we are God's children.*

You need to understand that a dream is about faith and trusting your thoughts. You need to trust and believe in your dreams and your plan. That is the way you will achieve your future. Do not be ashamed to share your dreams with others. Do not be afraid to do a new thing. Everything starts as a new thing at some point in time. Fear is the greatest enemy which will stop you from progressing.

> *The greatest enemy of your dream is the fear to failure. Failure is not failing it means you need more experience on your journey to success. If you quit, that is failure.*

You must believe that God is in your side and know that He will fight for you and protect you. God loves you and He wants you to be successful - that is why He will protect you.

> *Isaiah 54:17 - No weapon formed against you shall prosper,*
> *And every tongue which rises against you in judgment*
> *You shall condemn.*
> *This is the heritage of the servants of the Lord,*
> *And their righteousness is from Me,"*
> *Says the Lord.*

God's purpose is to bless you and condemn anyone who will go against you because He loves you so much. God cares about you so much - that is why you are not supposed to fear anything.

> *Genesis 12:2 - I will make you a great nation;*
> *I will bless you*
> *And make your name great;*
> *And you shall be a blessing.*
> *[3] I will bless those who bless you,*
> *And I will curse him who curses you;*
> *And in you all the families of the earth shall be blessed.*

18) Keep your focus.

You need to keep your focus on your dream. Do not allow anyone to force you to change your mind or change your focus on your dream. Keep your focus on your passion even if it may not be easy. If you keep your focus, you will keep moving forward. When you have a dream, you need to keep doing what helps you to keep thriving with your dream. You must know the people who make you lose your focus. You need to avoid those people to keep moving on with your dream.

You need to set up goals. Goals are a good way for you to keep moving on and to know what you are doing and how you are moving on and know what you are supposed to do. All throughout your life, you need to focus on your dream. Without focus, you may keep talking about your dream, but you will never change your life or achieve anything regarding your dream.

5 THINGS THAT MAKE YOU LOSE FOCUS

Friends

Some friends may want to spend time with you and before you realize it, no goals or tasks are accomplished by the end of the day. You find out they have taken away your time for nothing. Others may want to go out with you and spend your money. They just need you to buy things for them like drinks and food. That will cause you to keep losing focus regarding your dreams. You keep spending time and resources on them. Friends like that makes you lose focus on your future. You need to know that people like that may not have dreams or goals. You need to discern the friends you should choose for your own life. Certain people could put you in their own trouble. If you are hanging out with people who don't have any dreams, they will minimize or eliminate your dream. Spend your time with the right friends who are supporting your dreams and friends who are already successful. You can learn from them and they can help you to succeed.

Social media

During this time in history and throughout the whole world, people are losing focus because of social media. It seems to take way our time. Everyone is on social media. If you cannot manage your time well, you can lose sight of your dream by spending all your time on social media. Currently all social media is available right in our hands through our cell phones. Do not spend all your time on your cell phone. Some people spend more time on their cell phone following others. That will not help you to achieve any dream or keep your focus. Do not read your messages or text any one when you are in the meeting with great people. That will cause you to lose your focus to listen. That can cause you to lose the next invitation. If you keep checking your phone, it will look disrespectful to other people. You should honor others. Do not use your phone in a meeting. When you are meeting with someone, turn off your phone. Keep your focus on him because that is the important. That is why you are in a meeting with him. You need to listen and keep your focus. It will help you to listen and perhaps you will be granted another meeting. But if you do not focus on the meeting, you will not get another chance for another meeting. Keep your focus. Do not allow anything to take way your focus when you are meeting with successful people.

Television

Some people spend time watching television and forget their focus. Watching television within reason is not bad thing, but do not be on the television more than three hours per day. You need to manage your time. In my house, I did not put a television in my living room. If I want to watch television, then I go to my children's sitting room. That is the way to help me not spend more time watching television.

Other people spend more time on video games. To play video games is not a bad thing, but do not be addicted to video games. If you want to play some games, play for a limited time. Every moment spent playing might kill your focus on your dream.

Laziness

Laziness is the enemy of your dreams. If you like to sleep and keep relaxing and continually doing nothing, it will not help you regarding your dream. The proof of focus on your dream is to keep working hard. Some people like to keep talking about their dream, but they are not doing anything because of their laziness. Lazy people like to keep talking about their dreams, but they do nothing. Lazy people like relaxing and sitting down doing nothing so that is why they have nothing. Do something. If you do not have what you want, you can be certain that no one will just give it to you. You need work for it. Everything you need requires you to work for it. That is why we have many people in prison. They wanted to be successful, but they did not spend their time working for their future dream. They wanted to be successful overnight and get stuff the easy way.

Do not think other people will work and you get the benefit. That is why governments establish laws in order to protect people and their belongings. If you are lazy and you want to take someone else's belongings, you will be punished. Work hard for your own life. Do not be lazy. Use your hands to make your own income and God will bless the work of your hands.

Psalms 90: 17 – May the favor of the Lord our God rest on us; establish the work of our hands for us yes, establish the work of our hands.

Lack of Forgiveness

Lack of forgiveness keeps you thinking about others and then you forget about your focus. If you do not forgive others, that will make you lose your focus. By continually thinking about the wrong things that have happened in your life or you keep talking about the wrongs you have suffered from others breaks your focus. Forgiving others helps you to forget about the wrong things other people did to you. You cannot be free if you keep other people on your mind.

> Nelson Mandela said, "Forgiveness does not make you weak. It sets you free. If you do not forgive, you imprison yourself forever."

You need to have a free mind in order to help you to thrive with your dreams. That will make it possible for you to keep focusing on your dreams

Lack of Having Goals

If you do not have goals, you will not know where you are and where you are going. Goals help you to keep focus and to know what has been done, where you are, and where you will be going. You cannot know for sure if you are keeping your focus if you do not have goals. You must have very clear goals to track your progress.

19) Learn to honor.

You need to honor God and His principles. People who do not change often do not honor the law of God. God has commanded us to honor the law of God and to obey His law. That how we will be productive.

Deuteronomy 28:1 – If you fully obey the Lord your God and carefully follow all his commands, I give you today, the Lord your God will set you high above all the nations on earth.

You need to honor the people who are greater than you. That is the command of God. That is why many people are not successful. If you disrespect great people, you lose the chance to be successful. You cannot have favor with the people you dishonor.

Exodus 20:12 – Honor your father and your mother, so that you may live long in the land the Lord your God is giving you.

If you need to be great, learn how to honor great people. People will more likely support someone who will be willing to give honor to them and to respect them. Even God wants people to honor Him. No one wants to be with a person who cannot listen and follow the rules. All employers are looking for someone who can listen to them and follow instructions. To do what you have been told to do is the proof of honor.

Dr. Mike Murdock says, "Honor is the key to access and honor is the prediction of your future."

Honor will give you an opportunity to access great people. When you are with great people, show them honor and respect. That is a great way you can receive another opportunity for the next appointment.

Stupid people are people who are arrogant, but they impute in their mind and even in their pocket, but they're still proud.

6 THINGS CAN MAKE YOU LOSE
AN OPPORTUNITY

Dishonor: When you dishonor great people, you will lose an opportunity you were supposed to have. As you show great people the honor they deserve, you will get more chances to be around them. As you are around them, you will be able to learn from them and they will support you to be successful like them.

Disrespect: Lack of respect to anyone will cause you to lose access. No one will give you opportunity to be around him or her when you disrespect him. Everyone loves someone who shows respect.

Disobedience: Refusal to obey your leaders will cause you to lose an opportunity. All great people observe who will obey their commands. If you cannot obey, you are not qualified to be around them.

Pride: Pride is believing in yourself without listening to others. You need to be humble and listen to others if you want more opportunities from others. No one wants to be with someone who is proud. Pride is a lack of humbleness.

Arrogance: Not only is arrogance disrespectful, it means that you do not care about others. Arrogance proves that you care only about yourself and you cannot follow any instructions from others. That will make you lose an opportunity. Learn to obey and to honor others. It is a great way to keep other people with you and help you with your dream. You may be smart and have received a diploma from a great school, but if you are not humble, you may lose all the opportunities you should have. Humbleness in the greatest way to greatness.

Do not follow instructions: If you cannot follow instructions from your boss or great people, you lose an opportunity. When you are around successful people, you need to know about their protocol. You need to follow their instructions. If you cannot follow their instructions, you are disrespecting them. Then you will lose all the chances you have been given from them. Learn what your boss likes, and you will soon attract favor from him. Following instructions is proof of honor.

20) Keep doing what is right for your dream.

You need to keep following your goals and do what is right for your dream. Some people keep moving around because they think they are doing the right thing for their dream. You need to make sure you are doing the right thing which will keep you moving forward with your dreams. Do not keep doing something that will not support your dreams. That is why many people in life fail. They do not focus on their dreams. Your dream is your future. If you do not do right things, you will lose the right future.

21) Keep fighting your own battle.

To achieve your dream is not easy. You need to fight to keep moving on. No one will fight for you. You will have to fight for yourself. Everything has a price. You need to pay to get it. Focus with your own mind to have the right thoughts. Remove fear from your mind. You need to fight wrong thoughts - they are a deceitful enemy. You need to win in your own mind before you win outside. To win in your life is to keep doing right things - that is the first step of success.

22) Do what is important for your dream.

You will have different ideas but do what is right for your dream. You will meet many people who have different thoughts, but you must do what is the most important for your dream. You need to ignore those people who discourage you - that is only the way you can keep going forward. I have met many people who have told me that I could not succeed but I did not believe them. I kept doing what was important for my dream. No one knows where you are going more than you. Keep doing what is right for your dream.

23) Grow your faith.

Faith is the substance of things we hope for and the evidence of things not seen. Do not give up believing on your dream. You will be who you want to be if you have faith in your dream. God will help you if you trust Him. As you believe in your dream that is the proof that you will get where you are going. You are where you are because you believe what you believe.

Hebrews 11:1 - Now faith is confidence in what we hope for and assurance about what we do not see. This is what the ancients were commended for.

By faith we understand that the universe was formed at God's command, so that what is seen was not made from what was visible.

You need to grow up in your faith. That is how you will be able to achieve your dream. The proof of faith is to talk about your dream. You need to share your dream with others. That gives you the confidence to achieve your dream. You must

trust God. He is the one who can help you achieve
your imagination.

> *Ephesians 3:20 – Now to Him who can do immeasurably
> more than all we ask or imagine, according to his power
> that is at work within us.*

24) Learn from your pain.

Everything you have been going through is your experience.
Your experience is an education. Do not think everything you
have going through is specifically against you. Sometimes
God allows you go through some challenges so that you can
learn from that challenge. You will not see the will of God if
you do not see His goodness in your life.

> *John 11:4 – When he heard this, Jesus said, "This sickness
> will not end in death. No, it is for God's glory so that
> God's Son may be glorified through it."*

Pain is the proof of wrong things going on which require a
change. Through the pain we have experienced, we learn more.
Through the pain we have experienced, we change.

Do not allow the pain of what you are going through stop
you from moving on. You can change your response to pain.
You can heal and facilitate healing for others. Do not allow
pain to take your joy away.

> *I will not allow my pain to take away my joy.*

THREE WAYS TO LEARN

What you hear: People learn according to what they hear.
Be aware that listening to information long enough can
change your mind. That is why you need to listen to others

who have a life-giving message. That is how you can change your life.

> *Romans 10:17 - Consequently, faith comes from hearing the message, and the message is heard through the word about Christ.*

What you see: You can do what you see other people have done, you can learn from them. Your eyes relate to your mind. What you see is possible to achieve. Your eyes help you to imitate others. Everything you see that could possibly help you helps your mind will accept so you can achieve it.

Experience: Everything you have been going through may be painful, but it has given you a unique experience. It may be useful one day as you minister to others. What you have going through in any situation, that is your message.

25) Take time to pray for your dream.

You need to pray for your dream. God is the one who is able to help you and give you anything a human being cannot give you. He knows what you need, and He cares about you. Take time with God. He is your Creator. He knows why you are here to spend time with Him. You will know why you have been created. He is the only one who can make you self-sufficient.

> *Psalm 139:1-6 - Lord, you have examined me and know all about me.*
> *You know when I sit down and when I get up.*
> *You know my thoughts before I think them.*
> *You know where I go and where I lie down.*
> *You know everything I do.*
> *Lord, even before I say a word,*
> *you already know it.*

You are all around me in front and in back
and have put your hand on me.
Your knowledge is amazing to me;
it is more than I can understand.

After I left my country as a victim of civil war, I lost everything. My father, who I hoped would live for many years, died. I was hopeless. I spent time praying and reading the Bible. That is how I restored my life. You need to take time to think about your life. If you do not know where you are going, pray. Ask God to show you and read your Bible. You will find your answers in the Bible.

Chapter 9: Make a Difference

CHAPTER 10

Legacy

You need to think and plan your legacy. Legacy is what you will leave behind after you are gone. After you are done with your life on this earth, what you will leave behind for others is your legacy. Everything you do, you are doing for others. People will remember you according to what you did for them, not just what you have said.

> *Dr. Mike Murdock says, "People will remember you according to the problems you have solved or the problems you have created."*

For everything you do, think about what will happen when you are gone. When you are no longer here on this earth, how will people remember you? What you leave behind is how you will be remembered. While you are living, you still have a chance to change your life and impact others too. As you support others, there is the hope that you can leave a legacy behind.

4 Things you can do to leave a legacy behind

1) Do what you like to do.

This is what God has planned for you to do. You will be remembered according to what you did and not just what you have said. Many people speak well but you need to be a person who acts upon what you have said. Don't do things because other people have been doing it. Do what you want to do because you enjoy it. That is how you can do great things in your life. You will attract what you are born to do. You will be remembered for what you did with your passion. Your passion is your calling – the thing you were born to do. The proof of your calling is your love for it. It may be hard or it may be easy to you. You need to find out your purpose in life. That will help you to discover your legacy - what you will leave behind for the next generation.

2) Write down your dreams.

While you are still living, discover your dreams and what you need to accomplish in your lifetime. Find out what your dream is. What is your vision of the future? You have been created in the image of God. Do not be afraid of anything or anyone. You can achieve your great dream and leave a great dream for the next generation. It doesn't matter what you have been going through - you can still be great and achieve great things.

Find out in your heart what you love to do. Do it with joy without compromise. That is your legacy that you will leave to others. Do what you can to achieve your dream. You need to write down your dream. That is how you can be great in your life and be able to leave a legacy for others. Write down everything you are dreaming. Don't give up on your dream.

Keep trying and follow your dream. You will be able to achieve your dream and leave your legacy to others after you are gone.

3) Support others.

Be unique by supporting others. Don't live a selfish life. Don't think that you cannot help. Everyone can do something to support others. Don't think that you cannot serve others because you are not rich, or you are not successful. You just need enough to be able to make a difference. People don't always need money for help. People may need your services more than the material things you could give them. You can give them your time or service. Be willing to solve the needs of other people.

Dr. Martin Luther King, Jr. said, "Not everybody can be famous, but everybody can be great, because greatness is determined by service."

Use your knowledge and your ability to serve others with gratitude. That is how you will be able to change more lives. You will be an example to others as a part of your legacy. You can be remembered according to your service. Your service may change many lives. You need to know that a great thing in life is to serve others.

It's one thing to be something great but to be successful is to show how much you care about others.

To serve others will open more doors for you and make you great. Many people think that being served will make them special. If you want to be great, learn how you can serve others. All great people are serving others. Successful people are the people who are able to serve others. Some people think that having enough money will make you great and successful. But no one will remember you if you do nothing with your wealth. Learn how you can give back to others. People will remember you even though you are no longer here.

Matthew 23:11 – the greatest among you will be your servant.

I have been serving my community now for twelve years as a volunteer and as a senior pastor with different challenges. But when I see how people enjoy the services, I give them, my heart is full of happiness and joy. I forget all the other challenges I have been going through. You are here to be a blessing for others.

4) Write a book.

Your life is short. One day you will leave this life so you will need to let the younger generation know what your experiences were on this earth. Share what you have been going through and how other people may learn from you. Write down how you can help them in their time. You need to put together your thoughts. The great gift God has given to you is your thoughts. Everything you can imagine can become reality if you put your time into it. But many people do not care about their thoughts. God gave you your mind. It is a special engine that God has given to you. Write down any unique ideas you have. When other people read your book, they will know you existed. You can teach them and guide them even after you have died. You can speak into someone's life and inspire change in others.

You do not need to write a great book. You need to put together your ideas so other people can read and understand about what you have been writing. We learn from other people who have died before we were born, because they wrote down their ideas. That is why writing is important for you. I encourage you to write a book so then people will know who you are. Even after you have died, we will still have your mind speaking to us.

5) Compose a song.

If you want people to remember you, use your gift and do what you love to do. If you are able to compose a song, that will help you to leave a legacy. When people sing your song, they will remember you and you can still make people happy even when you are no longer living.

6) Have children.

When you have children, they are your greatest legacy you can leave on this earth. If you cannot have children on your own, you can adopt one. When you are no longer here, someone will remain who can share your legacy with others. Your children are your blood. Even after you have died, your blood will still be living. To raise another human being is an amazing gift you can give back to this world. To raise another human is an amazing legacy you can leave to the community.

7) Use your gift correctly.

God has given to you an amazing gift you can use to change the world and to support each other. In this world people have different gifts. As you use your gift, you are impacting and empowering more lives. Some people have the gift of invention. Anything you can invent is your legacy.

Steve Jobs invented Apple computer and the iPhone – that is his legacy. Anyone who uses an iPhone will remember this great man of invention in industry, Steve Jobs.

Dr. Martin Luther King, Jr. had the gift of speaking about his ideas. With his gift, he was able to help civil rights and bring justice to American society with his encouragement and fearlessness.

Steve Harvey, with his gift of comedy, has changed his own life and impacted many lives.

In this world people have different gifts. You need to know your gift. Your gift has been designed by God but will be discovered by you. You are the only one who can discover your gift. What is your gift? That gift you have is not for you alone. It is the gift God has given to you that you may be able to make an impact on this world in your lifetime and beyond.

Chapter 10: Legacy

CHAPTER 11

My Mission

After I lost everything and fled my country, I lost my father who was my hope. I lost my home. I did not know how my life would turn out, but through praying and reading the Bible, God restored my hope. God used other people to support me. I decided that I would help others as much as I could according to my ability. That is how I have started Churches and Organizations to help other refugees like me. We have churches in refugee camps in Kenya, Uganda, and Indianapolis. Every year I go back to the refugee camps and into the villages helping people who are still living life the way I used to live. I support their different needs and help them to build churches.

At times during my past, I was hopeless. I didn't even have a high school diploma. I did not know my future. I started to read the Bible which was where I was getting hope. As a person who has been a refugee and a survivor of civil war, I have a goal to bring Bibles to refugees. When I went into the refugee camps, I donated Bibles to the refugee community. Many of them have been living in the refugee camps for more than ten years. The Bible is the best gift I can give to anyone who is hopeless and struggling with life. With the Bible, you can find your hope. That is where I feel that I can support people who are struggling with life. I really need people who can continue to partner with us. We want to bring hope to the hopeless.

When I was growing up, I did not have school materials. I used to go to school without pen or paper. When my father bought a pencil, he used to cut it into four pieces and give each boy one piece of pencil. I remember my first class. It was under the trees. Now when I see the children there, I remember how I had grown up. That is why I want to keep supporting people who are struggling with life like I had struggled. I do not want to forget where I came from.

You can change the world by changing one person.
Mother Theresa

I am so proud of my wife Clementine N. Musinga. She has been supporting me so much. Without her I could not be who I am today. She understands my passion and my calling. She has been supporting me financially and even encouraging me when I am weak. Sometimes I tell her how we are struggling with our ministry. She tells me to keep trusting God: one day you will be successful. She is at my right hand always. She is the number one person to understand my passion and continues to support me.

Teaching girls how to use a sewing machine.

None of these young girls has been to school.

In many African communities, parents are not able to pay their children's school fees. Sadly, some do not understand the importance of an education. Others still have traditional views and do not believe girls should go to school. Thus, many girls and women are uneducated. Now we are trying to help young ladies who are less than eighteen years old and not attending school to learn how to sew. This will lead to a viable career and hope for their future. We hope to prevent them from getting swept into the sex trafficking business. There are currently girls in our Ugandan Refugee Program, as seen above standing with their instructor. Yet they only own 1 sewing machine. Join us in improving the economic sustainability for these young ladies by donating $100 to purchase a sewing machine. You can change the direction of an entire community through your donation. You can support us by going to our website: www.gracetmindy.com or writing a check to Grace Tabernacle Ministries and put "Sewing Machine" in the memo of the check.

CHAPTER 12

Give Thanks

I am taking this time to thank all the people who have been helping me in my life. I didn't know how my life would be. But by other people helping me and teaching me in different ways, my life has been changed. As you read this book, please always think of how you can be a blessing to someone. Always help other people if you can. That is one of the great things you can do in this world. Don't think that anything you do for others is too small. Anything you do for another is a great gift. You can change someone's life by finding out about their needs. I appreciate the people who have been supporting me with my dream.

I am taking this time to give thanks to my parents. My father was a great father and a great husband. He raised nine children even though he was poor man. He tried his best to make sure he took care of his family. I learned from him how to be a good father and work hard for my family. We had six boys and three girls in my family. He always spoke words of encouragement and how you can be successful if you work hard. He always told us the importance of education, how we need to be nice to our mother, and take care of our sisters. I

Rev. Raban Rupande & Pastor Ramu Nyirankema

was child number five in my family. His was sick for a short while before he died. His final words were to always help your family and take care your siblings and your mother. After he passed away, I started to take care of my younger siblings and my mother. We moved to Kenya then we moved to America.

I built a house and gave my mother her own room. She is my hero. I wish my father could be here. He would see how much we have thrived. She taught us, "You may not have enough, but be nice to your family." Teach good words of hope to your children and they will not forget what you tell them, even when you are no longer living with them. They will achieve what you wish for them.

My mother was a prayer warrior woman of God. She taught us how to pray, fast, and to obey the law. After our father passed away, we stayed with my mother. We spent many nights going hungry, but she told us to keep trusting God.

"One day God is going to bless us and change our family's life." She told us, "Don't steal or do any wrong thing, because if you need anything, you must trust God." She taught me and my siblings how to trust God. I appreciate my siblings. They have supported me with my dream more than I can tell you.

I appreciate my wife, Clementine N. Musinga. She has supported me in my life. She is my everything. She loved me when I didn't have anything. We started this journey together as a young refugee couple. We struggled together. When I told her about my dream, she believed me and supported me

as much she could. I was working hard - sometimes two or three jobs. I didn't have much time to spend with her, but she was very patient with me. She raised my five children while working two jobs. She is a wonderful woman and the greatest gift God has given to me.

Proverbs 18:22 – He who finds a wife finds what is good and receives favor from the Lord.

I give thanks to the Wildwood Baptist Church members at East Moline, Illinois. They have been a great blessing to me and my family since we arrived in America. I was new in this country. I didn't know anyone who could teach me how to start living as a newcomer refugee in a new country. Wildwood Church members took the time to teach about life in America. I didn't know how to drive. I was taking the bus going to work. My wife and I took three buses to take our daughter to daycare so that we could be able to go to work.

Wildwood Church members bought a minivan for my family. That was my first car! In fact, it was the first car that anyone in my father's family had ever owned. Wildwood

Church members taught me how to drive especially Mike Gray, Julie Gray and Cori Streight. They used their cars to teach me how to drive. God bless them as they risked their lives for me. I really appreciate how these people have made an impact in my life. You can make a difference in someone life. You may think that you are helping with something small, but it can make a great big impact in someone's life. When I moved from Illinois to Indianapolis, I went to plant a church there. The Wildwood Church has been supporting my mission for four years.

Brother Mike Gray took time to teach me about cars. This was my first car but I didn't know anything about cars at all. I didn't know how to drive or anything about changing the oil. He was teaching me how I need to make sure the car has engine oil and coolant. He took his time teaching me how to drive. I used his car to practice how to drive. I asked him if I can put gas into his car since he was helping me so much. But he said no because he was here to help me. I had never seen a man as kind as Mike Gray. I remember I met him when I was invited to a church to share my testimony.

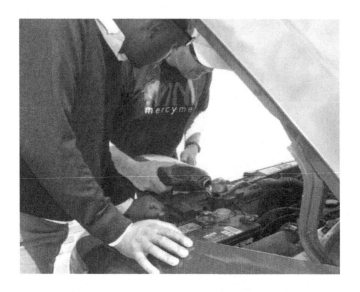

America was brand-new to me - I had been here only three weeks. He gave me an invitation to visit his church, Wildwood Baptist Church, the next week. I visited his church and we have been friends ever since. Brother Mike, you are such a great blessing in my life. And because you have changed my life, now I am better able to help other people. The best way for me to pay you back, Brother Mike, is to pay it forward and help our community.

Five months after arriving in America, Brother Mike took me to the DMV for the test. I passed the test! I got my driver's license! I was so happy - more than I can tell you. This was the best day of my life. I was so happy. I remembered the days when my wife and I were taking the bus to work – not just one bus but three buses to take my daughter to day care. Every day I was taking six buses with my daughter to take her there and bring her back home! Thank you to Mike and other people who have invested their time in my life. You have changed my life more than I can tell. Since that time, I started teaching other refugees how to drive. It is one of the basic things for how to start life in America.

Mike Gray and me
This is my favorite picture in the journey of my life.
It's the day when I got my driver's license.

I thank Cori Streight and Julie Gray. They taught my wife how to do the shopping and they gave us rides to go shopping. They spent so much time with us. My wife struggled with learning English, but they were patient with her. They came to our house and asked us how they may help us and kept checking on how we were doing. They made us feel more welcome and feel more comfortable in the new community. Thank you Gray family and Cori family for being my first American friends who entered into my house. It was a great blessing to have you in my house and it means a lot to my heart.

Cori and me

Mike Gray and me

These photos were taken when I came to the United States of America. I was new in this country when I met two families – the Mike Gray family and Cori family. They spent time with us and taught us different things. We didn't know anything. It means a lot in our hearts about how these two families have spent time with us. They made us feel more welcome in America. They helped us to integrate into society. They gave us rides and taught us how to shop for groceries in different stores, how to do shopping and especially how to use a card to pay for bills or shopping. We didn't know how to pay with a card, food stamps, or a debit card. Again, thank you Julie and Cori for teaching my wife to do the shopping. Now she teaches other refugee women what you have taught her and for what you did for us. We have had a lot of help in the refugee community.

Enos Morris has made an impact in my life. He likes the restaurant called Bishops. He took me and my family to this restaurant with Mike and Julie Gray. Then he told me, "I like your family. Always take care of your family as the number one thing in your life. Your family must have priority over everything that you want to do." He reminded me of my father because that was the last words my father told me, "Always take care of your family." I always thank him for how he showed me kindness when I was a stranger. He made an impact on me. You can make a difference in someone's life by showing him great love. He didn't know me, but he showed me great Love.

Mr. Enos Morris with my family
It was a great joy to spend time with someone who lives you.

Angie Nicolas, I really appreciate your generosity.

First of all, God is so good. God called me to become a minister and plant a church in Kenya while I was a refugee there. My wife and I didn't have any money to build a church. I was working in the restaurant for twelve hours every day, seven day a week. I rented a small place. I got a loan to build the church roof. I didn't know how I was going to be able to pay this loan. I took it by faith, trusting only in God. Then after few months, I moved to America. Then one day, Pastor Ron ask me to share my testimony at Wildwood Baptist Church. I told them about my life as refugee. When I done, Angie Nicolas asked me about my name. She gave me a check! I wasn't expecting anything. I used that check to pay all the loans for the church. In the year 2016, I became a citizen of the United States of America. I started a mission in Kenya and Uganda. Angie was the first one to support my mission again. I am taking this time to tell you - Thank you so much, Angie, to you and your family for allowing God to use you and making an impact in our ministry. You are the first person who supported our ministry. I always pray for you and your family. I ask God to keep you safe and healthy and make you prosperous in your life. May God bless you and your family.

Rev. Emmanuel Musing & Dennis Ford - 2011

My brother Dennis and I are really close friends. It has been ten years since I met Dennis at a Wildwood Baptist Church bible study. When I had been in America for four months, I received an invitation to go to speak in Portland, Maine. The church booked a flight for me at Chicago O'Hare International Airport. Remember, this was the time when I didn't know how to drive, so I took a bus from Rock Island to O'Hare airport. The big challenge was how I would come back. I didn't know the right way to come back home. I didn't know if I would find the right bus. Thankfully, I was able to phone a friend. I called my friend, Mike Gray, to tell him that was worried that I would get lost on the way back home. It would be my first time going to Chicago. Mike told me that Dennis Ford and Brother Done would come to pick me up at the airport. When I came back, I was just following the other people. I didn't know where I was going. I didn't even know how to follow the signs. The moment that I stepped out past security, I saw Dennis and Done. I was so happy and felt safe. I was scared that I would be lost. But as soon as I saw my brothers, I was so full of joy and started laughing. I felt so peaceful in my heart.

Brother Done with Rev. Emmanuel & Clementine Musinga

Dennis, Brother Done, and I went to the restaurant. Dennis took to me to McDonalds. That was my first time to enter into a McDonalds restaurant and I really liked it. Since then Dennis and I have become great friends. He hired me on at his land keeping company. Then in 2012, I moved to Indianapolis. My brother Dennis was sad to see me go. He asked if I could stay Illinois - he would support me as much he could, but I had a calling to start a church in Indianapolis.

The Musinga Family with Dennis & Kim Ford

I had been separated from my mother for six years. After this long wait, my mother joined me in America. Dennis and his wife, Kim Ford, came to help me to welcome my mother. It was a great joy to see my mother again and to see how my friends Dennis and his wife came to support me.

One of my dreams was to visit Israel. My friend, Dennis, planned a trip to Israel. He paid everything for me and himself too. It was unbelievable! When he told me, I almost could not believe it. I was so happy - more happy than I can tell you. We had a good time on that trip.

I thank Masha for organizing this trip. It was amazing to be with the people who care about you.

I thank God for inspiring my brother Dennis to help to achieve one of my dreams to visit the Promised Land.

I am taking this time to give thanks to Crooked Creek Baptist Church. Since we have started our church, they have been hosting us. I will never forget how this church has supported my ministry. All members of our church are refugees. Many of them work in warehouses and receive government benefits. Many are living from paycheck to paycheck. I have been their pastor for seven years now. They have not been able to pay me any salary. I am a volunteer. We have been using this building for the church and refugee community meetings. Crooked Creek Baptist church has supported the Congolese refugee community in Indianapolis in different ways.

We have shared meals and have cook outs together. We also worship together at the same time. We feel more welcome in the Indianapolis community because of this church. This church has become where many refugee people can meet and see each other. During weekdays, everyone is busy with work and family, but this is our place where we meet on weekends and tell each other how our lives are now and how we can help one other. I really appreciate the leadership and members of Crooked Creek Baptist church and how they have been a great blessing to my community. Members of Crooked Creek

Baptist Church have been supporting my mission in Africa. It is a great blessing to be with people who love you and support your passion. I have really seen the love of God in this church.

It was great to bring both communities together.
We shared a meal and enjoyed visiting one another.

Crooked Creek has a breakfast program called Manna. They feed the community and run a food pantry. Thank you for what you have been doing for the community.

I really appreciate the secretary for the church, Joan. Since the first day I walked into the building, she has welcomed me with joy. I met Pastor Tom. I asked if we can have our own service in this building. Afterward, the board agreed that we could use this building. Joan is the one who in charge of scheduling all the events that happen in the church building. She has been great to working with and I really appreciate how we have been working with her. Any time I have events, I just call her, and she helps to plan everything. Joan, it is a great blessing to work with you.

Secretary Joan and her husband

I really appreciate how Joan has been working with us as she manages the building. She is a really amazing person to work with. God bless you for the work you have been doing for all these years.

Reverend Bob and Elizabeth Yount

A NOTE FROM BOB YOUNT

My name is Bob Yount. I am a retired pastor and founder of Sheepdog Ministries INC. I met Emmanuel in the summer of 2016 while I was interim pastor at Crooked Creek Baptist Church where Grace Tabernacle meets for worship. He shared with me his vision and passion for his Congolese people still living as refugees in Nairobi, Kenya. Emmanuel is a man with deep passion for God's work in the world. He has big ideas and big plans that are always pointing toward meeting the needs of people anywhere and everywhere.

Because of Emmanuel's passion and vision, Sheepdog Ministries was able to assist his mission to Nairobi that fall. Early in 2017 Emmanuel impressed me so much with his passion for the people and work in Nairobi that I decided to organize a mission team to go to Africa. In August of 2017 we traveled with Emmanuel to Kayole and Kasarani churches in the slum areas of Nairobi. There we, with Emmanuel's presence, were able to assist families, widows, and church leaders with teaching, worship, and finances.

Having established personal relationships with the leaders of the Nairobi churches, Sheepdog Ministries INC is now able to send financial assistance to children and widows living in Nairobi. We have been able to help widows start their own businesses, pay for school expenses of children, and in December of 2018 Sheepdog Ministries was able to provide Christmas for 200 Congolese refugee children in Nairobi.

Rev. Bob and his wife, Elizabeth Yount, have supported the Congolese community with great love and amazing passion. I am so happy to know this great man of God. He has given me good advice to support our Africa mission. The great thing is that they understand my dream and keep encouraging me so much.

Any time I have question or if there is anything that I don't understand, he is the first person I ask as my pastor.

I really thank Rev. Bob with Elizabeth and their granddaughter, Rebecca, for how we went together on the mission in Kenya. It was so great!

Pastor Sam & Kim Howard

Pastor Sam and Kim Howard are the pastors of Gathering Church. I knew them from Exodus Refugee Immigrant where I was working to welcome new refugees. Gathering Church members came as volunteers to help newcomer refugees. We became friends. They helped me when I was starting the church in Indianapolis. Pastor Sam and Kim are a great blessing to the refugee community in Indianapolis. They have opened their church and their house for the refugees. We have brought both churches together many times to learn more from them. They have visited many refugees homes and help them as much as they can. When you visit their church, you will find our children playing around and enjoying themselves. It feels so good to have their church as a home - it blesses my heart. I appreciate how Gathering Church has opened their hearts for the refugees. Gathering Church is not a big church, but their heart is so great and so big - more than you can imagine.

I remember two refugee boys came here without their parents. Kim asked me if these two boys could come and stay with them. She was worried about how the two boys were going to start paying bills without going to school. The boys stayed with Kim and Pastor Sam until they graduated from high school. This act impressed my heart.

Kim with my daughters, Chloe and Daniella

I thank all my friends who have been supporting me. When I was celebrating my citizenship, I was so happy to see all my friends who came to support me during my ceremony.

Kim, Emily and Vicky

These ladies had been a great blessing to me and my family and even to the refugee community.

Gathering and Grace Tabernacle Church

We had a service with both churches together. It was great. We enjoy bringing all the community together. This is great love.

I love to see how Pastor Sam and Kim's family are full of love for everyone. I wish every American family could learn more from him.

Grace Choir and Castleton United Methodist Choir

I am taking this moment to give thanks to Castleton United Methodist Church. This church has been supporting us in so many different areas. They have opened their building for the refugees. We have brought our church worship together and our choirs sang songs together. It was so amazing! I really like how the choir was taking care of our ministry with great love. We made more friends and helped one another.

We have shared our worship and culture. It was so great. I really appreciated these two communities working together.

John Perkins

I really appreciate my friend, John. He friended me on Facebook. He called me and asked if we could meet. He is the one who has created our relationship with Castleton United Methodist Church. We work together to bring both congregations together. He is a wonderful friend. He supports the refugee community with great joy. I really appreciate his kindness.

Pastor Laurent Muvunyi and Rev. Emmanuel

I appreciate how Pastor Laurent has been supporting me in different activities. He is such a great friend of mine.

Dave and Julie Pappas

I met Dave in school - he was my English teacher. I invited him to our church and then he invited me to his house and also to his church. We have become great friends with Trinity Church too. We have partnered with Trinity Church as we support the refugee community and teach them integration into American culture and learning how to navigate life in this new system.

Officer Allen and Rev. Emmanuel

As partners with Trinity Church and with other churches, we have taken time to teach the refugees about public safety. I thank Officer Allen because he has taken his time to teach our community about public safety.

I really appreciate how you have been supporting my mission. It was a great blessing to have people who can stand with you. You have been a great blessing to me

It was great to bring the community together and share about their similarities and differences while enjoying the meal together. I appreciated those who have opened their houses to the new community and have shown them great love. God bless you so much.

Michelle Bell

I really appreciate Michelle for being one of my really good friends who has been helping me and my ministry. She used to be my employer and she was a member of Trinity Church. She was on the team to help both these churches to grow their relationship. Then she hired me and my wife. She has helped me with different things, and she has given me great advice. Thank you so much, Michelle, for what you have done for me.

Julie and Dave, I don't have any words I can say to fully communicate how I appreciate your support. I can only say God bless you for your kindness.

Pastor Andy and Rev. Emmanuel with married couple

Pastor Andy is the pastor of Union Chapel United Methodist Church. He has been a great friend for a long time. I really thank him and the members of Union Chapel UMC for how they have been a great blessing to our ministry and to the refugee community. When I started the church, they have been supporting us. I remember how they helped me to buy instruments for the church and support our mission.

God bless you for what you have done in our ministry especially how you have been welcoming us in your church. It was so amazing to see how Pastor Andy came to our church when some of our church members were married. This great love was amazing to both communities.

ABOUT THE AUTHOR

Reverend Emmanuel R. Musinga

Rev. Emmanuel R. Musinga was born in the Democratic Republic of Congo. He is a husband and father of five children - four girls and one boy. He is the founder of Grace Tabernacle Ministries and has planted different churches. He was a refugee who fled his home country and was a victim of civil war. His life growing up in the village was filled with struggles. During his years as a refugee, his father passed way before Emmanuel had a high school diploma. He was going to school in the morning and worked during the afternoons. As a young man, Rev. Musinga was supposed to pay his school fees and pay for his brothers and sister as well. Additionally, it was his job to bring food home. He went hungry many times in order to afford to go to school. But he did not allow himself to be discouraged with his life. Instead he became a stronger man who pursued his passion and hope. He loves other people and supporting his community. He has a passion to help others to attain success. He believes everyone has dream and that everyone can be successful. Rev. Emmanuel Musinga believes that everyone has greatness in him.

ENCOURAGEMENT FROM REV. MUSINGA

You need only to know who you are. Pursue your gift. You can be who you want to be. No one will make you great, only you. You are only the one who knows yourself best.

CONTACT INFORMATION

Rev. Emmanuel R. Musinga

Tel: 327-531-9451

Email: graceministry6@gmail.com

Address: 18282 Rickety Dr., Westfield, IN 46074

Made in the USA
Columbia, SC
13 November 2020

24452630R00104